BROOKLANDS BOOKS

VOLKSWAGEN BUS · CAMPER · VAN 1954 · 1967

Compiled by
R.M. Clarke

ISBN 1 870642 21X

Distributed by
Brooklands Book Distribution Ltd.
'Holmerise', Seven Hills Road,
Cobham, Surrey, England

BROOKLANDS BOOKS

BROOKLANDS BOOKS SERIES

AC Ace & Aceca 1953-1983
AC Cobra 1962-1969
Alfa Romeo Alfasud 1972-1984
Alfa Romeo Alfetta Coupes GT.GTV.GTV6 1974-1987
Alfa Romeo Giulia Berlinas 1962-1976
Alfa Romeo Giulia Coupés 1963-1976
Alfa Romeo Spider 1966-1987
Aston Martin Gold Portfolio 1972-1985
Austin Seven 1922-1982
Austin A30 & A35 1951-1962
Austin Healey 100 1952-1959
Austin Healey 3000 1959-1967
Austin Healey 100 & 3000 Collection No. 1
Austin Healey 'Frogeye' Sprite Collection No. 1
Austin Healey Sprite 1958-1971
Avanti 1962-1983
BMW Six Cylinder Coupés 1969-1975
BMW 1600 Collection No. 1
BMW 2002 1968-1976
Bristol Cars Gold Portfolio 1946-1985
Buick Riviera 1963-1978
Cadillac Automobiles 1949-1959
Cadillac Automobiles 1960-1969
Cadillac Eldorado 1967-1978
Cadillac in the Sixties No. 1
Camaro 1966-1970
High Performance Camaros 1982-1988
Chevrolet 1955-1957
Chevrolet Camaro Collection No. 1
Chevelle & SS 1964-1972
Chevy II Nova & SS 1962-1973
Chrysler 300 1955-1970
Citroen Traction Avant 1934-1957
Citroen DS & ID 1955-1975
Citroen 2CV 1949-1982
Cobras & Replicas 1962-1983
Cortina 1600E & GT 1967-1970
Corvair 1959-1968
Daimler Dart & V-8 250 1959-1969
Datsun 240z 1970-1973
Datsun 280Z & ZX 1975-1983
De Tomaso Collection No. 1
Dodge Charger 1966-1974
Excalibur Collection No. 1
Ferrari Cars 1946-1956
Ferrari Cars 1962-1966
Ferrari Cars 1969-1973
Ferrari Dino 1965-1974
Ferrari Dino 308 1974-1979
Ferrari 308 & Mondial 1980-1984
Ferrari Collection No. 1
Fiat-Bertone X1/9 1973-1988
Ford Falcon 1960-1970
Ford Mustang 1964-1967
Ford Mustang 1967-1973
High Performance Mustangs 1982-1988
Ford RS Escort 1968-1980
Honda CRX 1983-1987
High Performance Escorts MkI 1968-1974
High Performance Escorts MkII 1975-1980
Hudson & Railton Cars 1936-1940
Jaguar Cars 1957-1961
Jaguar Cars 1961-1964
Jaguar Cars 1964-1968
Jaguar MK2 1959-1969
Jaguar E-Type 1961-1966
Jaguar E-Type 1966-1971
Jaguar E-Type V12 1971-1975
Jaguar XKE Collection No. 1
Jaguar XJ6 1968-1972
Jaguar XJ6 Series II 1973-1979
Jaguar XJ6 & XJ12 Series III 1979-1985
Jaguar XJ12 1972-1980
Jaguar XJS 1975-1980
Jensen Cars 1946-1967
Jensen Cars 1967-1979
Jensen Interceptor Gold Portfolio 1966-1986
Lamborghini Cars 1964-1970
Lamborghini Cars 1970-1976
Lamborghini Countach Collection No. 1
Lamborghini Countach & Urraco 1974-1980
Lamborghini Countach & Jalpa 1980-1985
Lancia Stratos 1972-1985
Land Rover 1948-1973
Land Rover Series II & IIa 1958-1971
Land Rover Series III 1971-1985
Lotus Cortina 1963-1970
Lotus Elan 1962-1973
Lotus Elan Collection No. 1
Lotus Elan Collection No. 2
Lotus Elite 1957-1964
Lotus Elite & Eclat 1974-1981
Lotus Turbo Esprit 1980-1986
Lotus Europa 1966-1975
Lotus Europa Collection No. 1
Lotus Seven 1957-1980
Lotus Seven Collection No. 1
Maserati 1965-1970
Maserati 1970-1975
Mazda RX-7 Collection No. 1
Mercedes 230/250/280SL 1963-1971
Mercedes 350/450SL & SLC 1971-1980
Mercedes Benz Cars 1949-1954
Mercedes Benz Cars 1954-1957
Mercedes Benz Cars 1957-1961
Mercedes Benz Competition Cars 1950-1957
Metropolitan 1954-1962
MG Cars 1929-1934
MG TC 1945-1949

MG TD 1949-1953
MG TF 1953-1955
MG Cars 1957-1959
MG Cars 1959-1962
MG Midget 1961-1980
MG MGA 1955-1962
MGA Collection No. 1
MGB Roadsters 1962-1980
MGB GT 1965-1980
Mini Cooper 1961-1971
Morgan Cars 1960-1970
Morgan Cars 1969-1979
Morris Minor Collection No. 1
Old's Cutlass & 4-4-2 1964-1972
Oldsmobile Toronado 1966-1978
Opel GT 1968-1973
Packard Gold Portfolio 1946-1958
Pantera 1970-1973
Pantera & Mangusta 1969-1974
Plymouth Barracuda 1964-1974
Pontiac Fiero 1984-1988
Pontiac GTO 1964-1970
Pontiac Firebird 1967-1973
High Performance Firebirds 1982-1988
Pontiac Tempest & GTO 1961-1965
Porsche Cars 1960-1964
Porsche Cars 1964-1968
Porsche Cars 1968-1972
Porsche Cars in the Sixties
Porsche Cars 1972-1975
Porsche 356 1952-1965
Porsche 911 Collection No. 1
Porsche 911 Collection No. 2
Porsche 911 1965-1969
Porsche 911 1970-1972
Porsche 911 1973-1977
Porsche 911 Carrera 1973-1977
Porsche 911 SC 1978-1983
Porsche 911 Turbo 1975-1984
Porsche 914 1969-1975
Porsche 914 Collection No. 1
Porsche 924 1975-1981
Porsche 928 Collection No. 1
Porsche 944 1981-1985
Porsche Turbo Collection No. 1
Reliant Scimitar 1964-1986
Rolls Royce Silver Cloud 1955-1965
Rolls Royce Silver Shadow 1965-1980
Range Rover 1970-1981
Rover 3 & 3.5 Litre 1958-1973
Rover P4 1949-1959
Rover P4 1955-1964
Rover 2000 + 2200 1963-1977
Rover 3500 1968-1977
Rover 3500 & Vitesse 1976-1986
Saab Sonett Collection No. 1
Saab Turbo 1976-1983
Singer Sports Cars 1933-1934
Studebaker Hawks & Larks 1956-1963
Sunbeam Alpine & Tiger 1959-1967
Thunderbird 1955-1957
Thunderbird 1958-1963
Thunderbird 1964-1976
Toyota MR2 1984-1988
Triumph 2000-2.5-2500 1963-1977
Triumph Spitfire 1962-1980
Triumph Spitfire Collection No. 1
Triumph Stag 1970-1980
Triumph Stag Collection No. 1
Triumph TR2 & TR3 1952-1960
Triumph TR4.TR5.TR250 1961-1968
Triumph TR6 1969-1976
Triumph TR6 Collection No. 1
Triumph TR7 & TR8 1975-1982
Triumph GT6 1966-1974
Triumph Vitesse & Herald 1959-1971
TVR Gold Portfolio 1959-1988
Volkswagen Cars 1936-1956
VW Beetle 1956-1977
VW Beetle Collection No. 1
VW Golf GTi 1976-1986
VW Karmann Ghia 1955-1982
VW Scirocco 1974-1981
VW Bus-Camper-Van 1954-1967
VW Bus-Camper-Van 1968-1979
Volvo 1800 1960-1973
Volvo 120 Series 1956-1970

BROOKLANDS MUSCLE CARS SERIES

American Motors Muscle Cars 1966-1970
Buick Muscle Cars 1965-1970
Camaro Muscle Cars 1966-1972
Capri Muscle Cars 1969-1983
Chevrolet Muscle Cars 1966-1972
Dodge Muscle Cars 1967-1970
Mercury Muscle Cars 1966-1971
Mini Muscle Cars 1961-1979
Mopar Muscle Cars 1964-1967
Mopar Muscle Cars 1968-1971
Mustang Muscle Cars 1967-1971
Shelby Mustang Muscle Cars 1965-1970
Oldsmobile Muscle Cars 1964-1970
Plymouth Muscle Cars 1966-1971
Pontiac Muscle Cars 1966-1972
Muscle Cars Compared 1966-1971
Muscle Cars Compared Book 2 1965-1971

BROOKLANDS ROAD & TRACK SERIES

Road & Track on Alfa Romeo 1949-1963
Road & Track on Alfa Romeo 1964-1970
Road & Track on Alfa Romeo 1971-1976

Road & Track on Alfa Romeo 1977-1984
Road & Track on Aston Martin 1962-1984
Road & Track on Auburn Cord & Duesenberg 1952-1984
Road & Track on Audi 1952-1980
Road & Track on Audi 1980-1986
Road & Track on Austin Healey 1953-1970
Road & Track on BMW Cars 1966-1974
Road & Track on BMW Cars 1975-1978
Road & Track on BMW Cars 1979-1983
Road & Track on Cobra, Shelby &
  Ford GT40 1962-1983
Road & Track on Corvette 1953-1967
Road & Track on Corvette 1968-1982
Road & Track on Corvette 1982-1986
Road & Track on Datsun Z 1970-1983
Road & Track on Ferrari 1950-1968
Road & Track on Ferrari 1968-1974
Road & Track on Ferrari 1975-1981
Road & Track on Ferrari 1981-1984
Road & Track on Fiat Sports Cars 1968-1987
Road & Track on Jaguar 1950-1960
Road & Track on Jaguar 1961-1968
Road & Track on Jaguar 1968-1974
Road & Track on Jaguar 1974-1982
Road & Track on Lamborghini 1964-1985
Road & Track on Lotus 1972-1981
Road & Track on Maserati 1952-1974
Road & Track on Maserati 1975-1983
Road & Track on Mazda RX7 1978-1986
Road & Track on Mercedes 1952-1962
Road & Track on Mercedes 1963-1970
Road & Track on Mercedes 1971-1979
Road & Track on Mercedes 1980-1987
Road & Track on MG Sports Cars 1949-1961
Road & Track on MG Sports Cars 1962-1980
Road & Track on Mustang 1964-1977
Road & Track on Peugeot 1955-1986
Road & Track on Pontiac 1960-1983
Road & Track on Porsche 1951-1967
Road & Track on Porsche 1968-1971
Road & Track on Porsche 1972-1975
Road & Track on Porsche 1975-1978
Road & Track on Porsche 1979-1982
Road & Track on Porsche 1982-1985
Road & Track on Rolls Royce & Bentley 1950-1965
Road & Track on Rolls Royce & Bentley 1966-1984
Road & Track on Saab 1955-1985
Road & Track on Toyota Sports & G T Cars 1966-1986
Road & Track on Triumph Sports Cars 1953-1967
Road & Track on Triumph Sports Cars 1967-1974
Road & Track on Triumph Sports Cars 1974-1982
Road & Track on Volkswagen 1951-1968
Road & Track on Volkswagen 1968-1978
Road & Track on Volkswagen 1978-1985
Road & Track on Volvo 1957-1974
Road & Track on Volvo 1975-1985

BROOKLANDS CAR AND DRIVER SERIES

Car and Driver on BMW 1955-1977
Car and Driver on BMW 1977-1985
Car and Driver on Cobra, Shelby & Ford GT40
  1963-1984
Car and Driver on Datsun Z 1600 & 2000
  1966-1984
Car and Driver on Corvette 1956-1967
Car and Driver on Corvette 1968-1977
Car and Driver on Corvette 1978-1982
Car and Driver on Ferrari 1955-1962
Car and Driver on Ferrari 1963-1975
Car and Driver on Ferrari 1976-1983
Car and Driver on Mopar 1956-1967
Car and Driver on Mopar 1968-1975
Car and Driver on Pontiac 1961-1975
Car and Driver on Porsche 1955-1962
Car and Driver on Porsche 1963-1970
Car and Driver on Porsche 1970-1976
Car and Driver on Porsche 1977-1981
Car and Driver on Porsche 1982-1986
Car and Driver on Saab 1956-1985
Car and Driver on Volvo 1955-1986

BROOKLANDS MOTOR & THOROUGHBRED & CLASSIC CAR SERIES

Motor & T & CC on Ferrari 1966-1976
Motor & T & CC on Ferrari 1976-1984
Motor & T & CC on Lotus 1979-1983
Motor & T & CC on Morris Minor 1948-1983

BROOKLANDS PRACTICAL CLASSICS SERIES

Practical Classics on Austin A 40 Restoration
Practical Classics on Land Rover Restoration
Practical Classics on Metalworking in Restoration
Practical Classics on Midget/Sprite Restoration
Practical Classics on Mini Cooper Restoration
Practical Classics on MGB Restoration
Practical Classics on Morris Minor Restoration
Practical Classics on Triumph Herald/Vitesse
Practical Classics on Triumph Spitfire Restoration
Practical Classics on VW Beetle Restoration
Practical Classics on 1930S Car Restoration

BROOKLANDS MILITARY VEHICLES SERIES

Allied Military Vehicles Collection No. 1
Allied Military Vehicles Collection No. 2
Dodge Military Vehicles Collection No. 1
Military Jeeps 1941-1945
Off Road Jeeps 1944-1971
V W Kubelwagen 1940-1975

BROOKLANDS
BOOKS

CONTENTS

BROOKLANDS BOOKS

ACKNOWLEDGEMENTS

Brooklands Books are works of reference for enthusiasts. Their purpose is to make available to current owners, stories that appeared about their vehicles when they were in production. We rely on the goodwill of the publishers of the worlds leading motor journals who for many years have generously allowed us to reissue their copyright road tests and other articles in this series. Our thanks go especially in this instance to the management of Autocar, Car and Driver, Car Life, Commercial Motor, Eastern Daily Press, Foreign Car Guide, Hot Rod, Mechanix Illustrated, Motor, Motor Life, Motor Trend, Popular Imported Cars, Road & Track, Safer Motoring, VW Transport Magazine and The World Car Guide.

Our thanks also go to Brian Screaton, the well known purveyor of Volkswagen literature, who not only encouraged us to tackle the Transporter, but went on to advise us and loan us valuable material which has been included. We were also able to persuaded him to pen a few lines of introduction and so we gratefully hand over to him.

R.M. Clarke

The 'People's Van' was perhaps a logical extension of the 'People's Car' philosophy for Volkswagen, but the inspiration for its design came from a Dutchman, Ben Pon. As well as being the first dealer to receive export Beetles, Pon sketched a design for a VW Van as early as 1947, inspired by the flatbed transport vehicles used in the Wolfsburg Factory. These had been designed by Major Ivan Hirst of the Military Government, whose task it was to re-start car production following the war-time devastation.

The idea was not immediately taken up, but after the initial problems of Beetle production were overcome, a prototype Van was produced in 1949, and production of the Bus, Kombi and Panel Van began in 1950. The vehicle (known officially as the 'Type 2') created an entirely new market and as a reliable and versatile workhorse, carved out a place for itself in Germany and beyond.

Official variations of the original design began in the early 1950's with the Ambulance, Fire-tender and Pick-up truck, as well as Camper conversions produced by firms such as Westfalia and Dormobile. Unlike the Beetle, the Type 2 came in almost any shape a buyer wanted, but even so, unofficial variations were countless! To keep up with demand an entirely new factory was opened in Hannover in 1956. The millionth Type 2 was produced in 1962, and by the end of its production in 1967, nearly 2 million had been built.

Affectionately known as the 'Bulli' in Germany, the early Type 2 was updated regularly and indeed used as a test bed for modifications later applied to other VW vehicles. For most of its life it was the top selling commercial vehicle in its class in Germany, and now nearly 40 years later its third generation cousin continues the 'box on wheels' design.

The 'Bulli' is fast becoming collectable, with knowledgeable owners exchanging talk of 'Barndoors' and 'Safari Windows'. Clubs for enthusiasts include the 'Split-Screen Van Club' in the U.K. and the 'Society of Transporter Owners' in the U.S.A. Members of both Clubs are, I am sure, not the only ones to appreciate the merits of Ben Pon's Inspiration.

Brian R. Screaton   October 1988
Cosby Leicester

Newcomer Sets High Standard

German-built 15-cwt. Van has Four-wheel Independent Suspension and Rear-mounted Air-cooled Engine : A Cab Heater and Other Refinements are Provided

by Laurence J. Cotton, M.I.R.T.E.

(Above) Stop-start tests were accomplished on a 1 in 4¼ gradient when carrying part load. The Volkswagen has a smart appearance with modern styling. (Right) The van is seen here approaching Ludgate Circus, with Holborn Viaduct in the background, during its trials in London traffic.

THERE are few power units, for light commercial vehicles, that can compare with the efficient operation of the Volkswagen four-cylindered horizontally opposed petrol engine. In its entirety, the 15-cwt. van is remarkable both in construction and performance, as I found during a series of tests, totalling over 200 miles in one day. Much can be said for the driving comfort in that I felt far from weary at the end of the run.

Having previously driven a Volkswagen in Germany, its liveliness with light load was not surprising, but trying the van with a 15-cwt. payload on home ground confirmed that it is speedy and economical, and well equipped, in its lowest ratio, to soar over the 1-in-4¼ gradient of Succombs Hill with power to spare.

In physical layout it is similar to the Volkswagen car, having the compact, four-stroke, overhead-valve petrol engine housed in a compartment at the rear. It is air cooled by a fan and a constant temperature is maintained by a thermostat which also passes a regulated flow of air over an oil cooler. No difficulties were encountered in cold-start tests after the van had been left out overnight on a parking ground during a period when several degrees of frost were recorded.

The engine is reached by lifting a

The wide forward-hinged door provides easy access to the cab, which has a bench-type seat. The heater duct is seen attached to the front panel.

hinged panel at the back of the body. In this compartment there are also the 6-v. battery, 8¾-gal. petrol tank and spare wheel, the latter being

housed on a shelf above the power unit. Accessibility to the dynamo, coil, distributor, carburetter and petrol pump, is excellent, which is to be expected with the small, flat engine being housed longitudinally in a compartment which is as wide as the body.

As my tests started before daybreak, I appreciated the built-in illumination of the engine bay when connecting the petrol lift pump to an auxiliary supply. This small attention to detail is found in many other parts of the van.

The clutch and four-speed synchro-mesh gearbox are attached to the front of the engine and the final drive is through a spiral-bevel gear to swinging half axles, and then through a secondary spur reduction gear in the hubs. The Volkswagen power and transmission units are thus compactly grouped and arranged for easy change or major repair. The engine, of 1.192-litres capacity, and a compression ratio of 6.2 to 1, develops 30 b.h.p. at 3,400 r.p.m.

Like the car, the commercial version, which is available as a van, eight-seater bus, ambulance and as a combination of a bus and van, is of semi-integral construction having a basic structure for all models but differing in the assembly of the upper sections.

The commercial versions are all forward-control types with the front axle situated directly below the full-width driving seat. Considering the 8-ft. wheelbase is about the same as many local-delivery electric vehicles, the suspension of the Volkswagen is extraordinarily good.

The independent front suspension units employ trailing links on laminated square-section torsion bars and the independent units at the divided rear axle have round-section torsion bars. Double-acting hydraulic shock absorbers are fitted at all wheels.

Good Suspension

Although tested with varying pay-loads up to 17 cwt. maximum, I found nothing to criticize in the springing, and even deliberate driving over a 4-in. kerbstone at 15 m.p.h. failed to " bottom " the buffers.

The wide cab doors, hinged at the front, give good access to the driving seat, but the gear and hand-brake levers projecting through the floor obstruct the driver so that he cannot get out on the near side without some difficulty. There is a speedometer-milometer which is the only instrument provided, the head lamp beam, traffic indicators, dynamo charging and oil pressure being indicated by lights on the facia panel.

No fuel gauge is provided, but the tank has a three-way tap affording a one-gallon reserve after the main supply is used. Although austere, the instrument-panel equipment is adequate for a van.

Built-in Heater

With the engine at the back of the body, the cab would be cold in winter without some form of heating. A built-in heater, therefore, forms standard equipment, hot air from the engine being suitably ducted to the cab.

This I found to be most effective within a few minutes of starting the engine, and the only possible fault that could be visualized is that fumes that are prone to emanate from an engine that has seen considerable service might also be forced into the cab. As it is, Volkswagen has provided an effective unit without additional cost.

The cab furnishing is severe, a compressed paper-board lining being used to window level, and, as already indicated, the instrumentation costs little. It is surprising, therefore, to

(*Above*) *The Volkswagen climbed Succombs Hill, carrying full load, without stopping on the* 1 *in-4¼ section. It is well geared for rapid local delivery and is economical under all conditions of load or duty.*

find swivelling glass vents and sliding windows in the doors, twin wind-screen wipers, and cab and interior lights in the body forming standard equipment.

The low engine position does not prevent rear doors being fitted to the van body, but on the model tested there was a 3-ft. 10-in.-wide opening with two doors at the near side and similar doors can be provided at the off side as an optional extra. For a 15-cwt. van the payload space of 141 cu. ft. in the main section of the body, plus another 21 cu. ft. over the engine bay, might invite overloading. The loading height, when unladen is 1 ft. 7 in.

After taking delivery of the van from V.W. Motors, Ltd., in London, I loaded 15-cwt. of ballast in the body and drove through the busiest part of the city to the suburbs. The engine idled and ran smoothly, but, like other Volkswagen models I have driven, could not always be guaranteed not to stall when pulling up sharply in traffic.

Although its acceleration, with load, could not equal that of the fast newspaper delivery vehicles, the van put up a spirited performance and with reduced payload it kept its place at the head of all other traffic.

Apart from being easy to control

in steering and general handling, the gear change was without fault and rapid movements of the lever evoked no protest from the box. It is preferable to pass through all four gears for the best acceleration with full load. On a quiet level stretch of road alongside the Thames I found the acceleration rate to be from rest to 30 m.p.h., 13.2 sec., and to 40 m.p.h., 22.7 sec.

No Wheel Locking

The maximum effort on the pedal failed to lock the wheels during braking, which is unusual for a vehicle of the light-van class. The Volkswagen has hydraulic braking which, when carrying full load, will stop the van in 43 ft., from 30 m.p.h., which corresponds to 0.7g. The excellent distribution of load, 18½ cwt. on the rear axle and 18 cwt. at the front, may have been contributory to the prevention of wheel locking although the brake frictional area corresponds to 81 sq. in per ton with this load.

Before starting consumption trials from Godstone, I tried the Volkswagen on Succombs Hill to verify the maker's claim that the van will climb a 1 in 4.3 gradient with full load. This it did without faltering, but I could not stage a stop-start trial on the 1 in 4¼ gradient without abusing the clutch. With an 8 cwt. payload, however, the result was quite successful. The van made no fuss when starting from rest on a 1 in 5 gradient with a 15-cwt. load and a passenger. It was well geared for general work.

Extensive fuel consumption trials

Volkswagen Consumption Tests

Load	Non-stop		One stop per mile		Four stops per mile	
	m.p.g.	m.p.h.	m.p.g.	m.p.h.	m.p.g.	m.p.h.
15 cwt.	28.7	at 31.2	25.7	at 31.6	19.1	at 27.1
8 cwt.	32	at 31.6	28.6	at 31.7	21.6	at 27.9
Empty	33.3	at 31.6	30.5	at 31.6	24.6	at 27.9

MODEL : Volkswagen 15-cwt. van.

WEIGHTS :

	Tons	cwt.	qr.
Unladen	—	18	0
Payload	—	15	0
Driver, observer, etc. ..	—	3	2
	1	16	2

DISTRIBUTION :

	Tons	cwt.	qr.
Front axle	—	18	0
Rear axle	—	18	2

ENGINE : V.W. four-cylindered horizontally opposed overhead-valve petrol engine; bore 77 mm. (3.03 in.) ; stroke 64 mm. (2.52 in.) ; piston-swept volume 1.192 litres (72.74 cu. in.) ; maximum output 30 b.h.p. at 3,400 r.p.m. ; R.A.C. rating 14 h.p.

TRANSMISSION : Through single-dry-plate clutch and four-speed gearbox, and spiral-bevel drive to open driving shafts with reduction gear in the hubs.

GEAR RATIOS : 3.60, 1.88, 1.23 and 0.8 to 1 forward ; reverse 4.63 to 1 ; rear-axle ratio 6.2 to 1.

BRAKES: Hydraulically operated to all wheels. Hand brake linked mechanically to rear wheels only. Diameter of drums 9 in. ; total frictional area 81 sq. in., that is, 44.4 sq. in., per ton gross weight as tested.

FRAME : Integral with body.

STEERING : Worm and cam follower.

SUSPENSION : Two square laminated torsion bars at front, individual solid torsion bars at rear. Double-acting hydraulic shock absorbers at all wheels.

ELECTRICAL : 6v. compensated-voltage-control system with 85-amp.-hr. battery.

FUEL CONSUMPTION : (a) Non-stop, 28.7 m.p.g. at 31.2 m.p.h. average speed ; (b) one stop per mile. 25.7 m.p.g. ; (c) four stops per mile, 19.1 m.p.g. ; that is, 52.4 gross ton-m.p.g. as tested (a), 46.9 gross ton-m.p.g. (b) and 34.8 gross ton-m.p.g. (c) giving a time-load-mileage factor of 1,633.

TANK CAPACITY : 8¾ gallons, range approximately 160-250 miles.

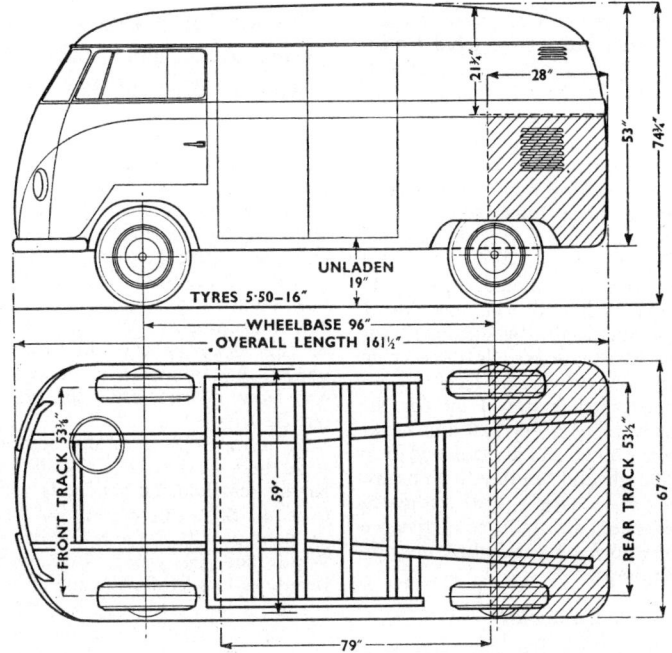

UNLADEN 19″
TYRES 5·50–16″
WHEELBASE 96″
OVERALL LENGTH 161½″
FRONT TRACK 53⅛″
REAR TRACK 53½″
59″
79″

ACCELERATION: Through gears, 0-30 m.p.h., 13.2 sec. ; 0-40 m.p.h., 22.7 sec.

BRAKING: From 20 m.p.h., 19 ft. (22.5 ft. per sec. per sec.) ; from 30 m.p.h., 43 ft. (22.5 ft. per sec. per sec.).

WEIGHT RATIOS: 0.823 b.h.p. per cwt. gross

weight as tested. Payload 41 per cent. o gross load.

TURNING CIRCLES : 37 ft. both locks.

MAKERS : Volkswagenwerk, G.m.b.H., Wolfsburg, Brunswick, Germany. Concessionnaire : V. W. Motors, Ltd., 7-9 St. James's Street, London, S.W.1.

---

were made, embracing varying degrees of load and making one- and four-stops-per-mile tests in addition to continuous running. The result of these trials is shown in the accompanying table, the speed for the one- and four-stops-per-mile tests being developed from the time the wheels were turning.

By running these trials early in the morning there were no traffic difficulties, and between 5.30 a.m. and 10 a.m. 18 runs were made with comparable conditions and reasonably equal average speeds. From the results it is apparent that the maker's claim for a consumption rate of 30 m.p.g. is not unreasonable at a steady speed with load. The course chosen was slightly undulating.

As I did not spare the engine or brakes during the local-service trials, the return of 19.1 m.p.g. carrying full load and stopping every ¼ mile is an economical figure. It is upon the results of these trials that I acclaim the Volkswagen engine to be above average in its efficiency. It is especially good for local deliveries because of its rapid " warm up " from cold, no engine heat being lost in a water-cooling jacket.

After 200 miles arduous work there was no increase in pedal travel, neither could the brake adjusters be taken up without binding the wheels. If competition is measured by the performance of the Volkswagen the standard is high.

Mobile Dispensary for the Desert

A FOUR-WHEEL-DRIVE long-wheelbase Land Rover forms the basis of a mobile dispensary which the British Red Cross Society are sending to Dubai for operation in remote areas of the Persian Gulf. It has been built and equipped by Messrs. Pilchers, ambulance specialists, 314 Kingston Road, London, S.W.20.

The bodywork, which incorporates an aluminium double-skin roof insulated with Isoflex, is well ventilated. Cupboards for drugs, dressings and other equipment are fitted along the off side, whilst on the near side there is a light alloy folding stretcher. Fresh water is carried in Polythene containers, and washing facilities are provided. Hooks are provided along the sides from which water skins can be suspended.

Additional accommodation is afforded by a tent fixed to the rear of the body. The tailboard forms a folding step.

Special mattress devices are provided for preventing the wheels from sinking in the sand when the unit is operating in the desert.

Mr. R. Pilcher explaining features of the dispensary to officials of the British Red Cross Society before it left this country for Dubai.

Eight Men in a Microbus

Volkswagen Covers 2,117¾ Miles at 32.2 m.p.h. and a Consumption Rate of 26.9 m.p.g.

A FEW days ago eight tired, hungry and unshaven men entered Folkestone at three minutes to midnight. Thus ended a 2,000-mile round tour of Britain in a Volkswagen Microbus.

The run, which was organized by the main Volkswagen agents in this country, was undertaken to show the economy of this vehicle when fully laden over a long distance, and to demonstrate the reliability of the 1.2-litre air-cooled engine. The total time from start to finish was 74 hr. 28 min. and during this time the engine was stopped for only two 10-minute periods, these being necessary to check the oil level.

A time schedule drawn up for the run embraced stops for fuel and meals at specific points, and a change of crew at Edinburgh and another at Glasgow on the way back. The estimated average speed for the whole distance was to be 26 m.p.h., including the prearranged stops.

Late Start

A reception for the crew had been prepared by C. and H. L. Blundell, Ltd., the Folkestone Volkswagen distributors, and as a result of its magnitude the run was not started until 9.30 p.m., the scheduled start time being 8 p.m.

A clear road up to and through London enabled a high road speed to be maintained and after a fuel stop in North London a fast run was made as far as Newcastle upon Tyne, by which time we were back on schedule.

By now it had become painfully obvious to the crew that the vehicle was not suitable for comfortable long-distance travel, in spite of its assets as a ferry vehicle. There are three rows of seats, and each presents its own peculiar climatic problems. The rear seat, which is directly in front of the engine, was so well heated as to be distinctly uncomfortable.

In the front seat the position was somewhat different, because the heater could not be used for long periods for fear of suffocating the back-seat passengers.

Between the devil and the deep blue sea were the passengers in the centre seat, who were getting neither direct heat nor direct fresh air, and remained well muffled with rugs and overcoats to keep out draughts. With the exception of the lucky two in the front seat, nobody had much legroom and sleep was more or less impossible throughout the trip.

So it was with a certain amount of relief that we arrived at Edinburgh as per the schedule and handed the vehicle over to a Scottish crew whose lot it was to continue to John o'Groats, Cape Wrath and Glasgow. Just north of Beauly a lorry travelling in the opposite direction shed a 10-ft. Christmas tree across the front of the bus and

neatly knocked off the fog lamp, in addition to smothering the windscreen with greenery.

Farther south, a 4½-in. nail successfully penetrated the near-side rear tyre and this necessitated a hurried wheel change in pouring rain. The punctured tyre was then entrusted to the care of the tender car, which up to that time had been faithfully following the Microbus. While the puncture was being repaired contact between the two vehicles was lost, but they re-met at Glasgow, where the original crew once more took over.

By the time Preston was reached we were 1½ hr. ahead of schedule and the tender car had been lost. The prearranged meal at Preston was not ready, so a hasty plate of fish and chips was grabbed and the nose was turned to Exeter, our next port of call.

Early Arrival

Exeter was also reached well ahead of schedule and far too early in the day to obtain any breakfast, but a meal was managed at Bodmin and various telephone calls established the fact that the tender car was still two hours behind us. It was decided not to wait for it and Lands End was reached an hour before our estimated time of arrival.

The last leg to Folkestone, which followed the A30 road for the most part, was made with only one short stop for fuel, and Folkestone was reached after a total running time of four hours under that originally set.

The total distance covered was 2,117¾ miles and for this distance 78½ gallons of fuel had been necessary. This gave fuel-consumption at the rate of 26.9 m.p.g.

Throughout the run only one pint of engine oil had been added and apart from the use of the spare wheel it had not been necessary to fit any of the spare parts which were carried in the bus. The total time for which the wheels were turning was 65 hr. 23 min., which gives an average running speed of 32.2 m.p.h.

Just for laughs, Tom tested Kombi's cornering, found it held on very well.

SPECIFICATIONS

MODEL TESTED:

Volkswagen Kombi (station wagon)

ENGINE:

4 cylinder, opposed, OHV, bore 3.31 inches, stroke 2.52 inches; piston displacement 72.74 cubic inches; brake horsepower 30 @ 3400 rpm; compression ratio 6.1 to 1

DIMENSIONS:

Wheelbase 96 inches; overall length 161½ inches; tread 53⅜ inches front, 53½ rear; width 70 inches; height 75 inches; weight 2,039 pounds; load space 162 cubic feet; standard tire size 5.50x16; gas tank 10½ gals

Top speed, 60 mph

This striking view shows how roomy and accessible the Volkswagen is.

vard appeal of a paratrooper's left boot or a pair of paint-splattered overalls. This is a purely functional workhorse and the designers obviously didn't give a damn whether it looked like an egg in a washing machine providing it did the work. And that it does.

The first time I saw one of these marmalade jars in full action was at LeMans. A group of California sports car men, three of them to be exact and their wives, arrived in one of these wagons for the race. After the race all six adults toured the race circuits of Europe in their Volkswagen Kombi with enough baggage and camera equipment to cause the Queen Mary to list. In Switzerland I met two Englishmen and their wives, plus two kids, who were doing the same thing, only this time I met them going over one of the highest passes in the Alps. Two Italian friends of mine used a Kombi for an African big game hunt as a mobile, in-the-field hotel. For the sportsman, it would be almost impossible to match unless he spent many thousands of dollars more for custom equipment. It has far superior traction and over-rough-terrain ability than any station wagon we build. It will almost go anywhere a Jeep will with but a few exceptions. It only weighs a little over 2,000 pounds and its air-cooled 30-horsepower Volkswagen engine will give better than 30 miles to a gallon and haul a load of 1,750 pounds while doing it.

The car I tested belonged to Jack Penn,

German-built by the makers of the Volkswagen and Porsche, Kombi costs $2,000.

MI Tests the VW Station Wagon

Call it a Kombi, a van or a bus, it's actually

the greatest thing of its kind.

THE greatest in the world would be one way of describing the Volkswagen station wagon—if there was anything around to compare it with. Actually, it's strictly a one-of-a-kind deal, like striped hair or a six-legged horse. It is the only station wagon I have ever seen that has enough up-and-down room and forward-and-aft space to take the station with you —if you want to.

Now, a lot of guys will claim that this VW doesn't look like a station wagon, that it looks more like a new-born Greyhound bus, but the fact is "station wagon" is a nebulous, looseleaf term that can be applied to many vehicles. This little beetle can carry eight people with ease to the 8:15 train and all their luggage for a world cruise. The big deal and why we are bring-

ing you this test, is that for what it is (you name it) it's unquestionably the world's greatest buy. The cost of the plain wagon which I tested is $1,995, delivered in New York. Officially the name is Kombi, van or bus. It could be called a station wagon or suburban when you get your license, even though you can just as easily call it a truck. It is as versatile as a steamship con man and twice as useful. If you are a stickler for deluxe equipment you can, for a grand more, buy this rig with a convertible roof and observation windows for high-riding squirrels.

To look at this rear-engine bingo wheel in its true perspective, a lot of facts jump out like Tarzan after Jane. You won't need a goat skin from the Beaux Arts in Paris to realize this rig has the chic and boule-

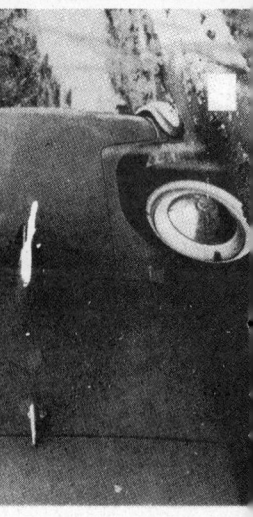

Like all Volkswagens, the power plant is an air-cooled, rear-mounted job, with four cylinders opposed. Its brake horsepower is 30 @ 3400 rpm.

Jack Penn demonstrates the interior roominess of the Kombi. Six adults and all their luggage can easily fit into the wagon for an extended trip.

Uncle Tom says the Kombi "will go anywhere and two feet further than any automobile made in the United States except the four-wheel-drive Jeep."

the Kombi speed is not much better than a fast walk but it will get there.

Patience is a European motoring trait, unknown over here. The average American driver would slit his throat if he had to go over the Alps in the average European low-powered family car. It's like walking upstairs pulling a bull moose. To the typical American, that underpowered, high-speed slow grind is similar to a nail scraping on a blackboard. In Europe it's the order of the day so no one thinks anything about it, especially as they are getting twice as many miles to the gallon (where gas may run as high as a dollar a gallon), compared with average American transportation.

For the price of one or two good bottles of whiskey you can buy enough Kombi fuel for a round-trip up the Alcan Highway after bear. This car will never appeal to the so-called suburban station wagon set because it looks too much like a truck. It should appeal, though, to the guy who is just interested in the best equipment, whether it's to take his brood to the beach or for a trip to the coast with all his earthly possessions including his TV set and the furniture. Paul Whiteman is thinking about buying one of these for a hunting car just to take to regular shoots. He would rig it up with an ice box, stove, gun racks, etc. This is just the thing for a rod and gun club to buy for the members as a mobile base or for field trial enthusiasts to carry a dozen or so dogs and equipment in. If it was just a little faster, what a job for pulling another Brinks holdup! First, you would put the armored car in the back. Then—oh, well, you know what I mean.

New Jersey foreign car dealer, Jack, a sports car race driver, uses this as his team car. It's big enough to carry all spare parts and tools plus extra tires and still provide enough room for three men to sleep in it in sleeping bags. With the exception of its plumbing facilities, which are strictly continental (meaning none), you could live in this bolt house for a year. The heater is good and, with the middle two-minute-removable seat, you could transport a full grown Kodiak bear, a baby elephant or a Steinway grand.

Some of our readers might well be in the market for such a tug. It's not fast, 60 at better than 50. If you are the type who collects kids everytime you turn over and have six or seven, then this tin envelope is perfect for that trip to camp, the beach or to the relief office. If you are the type who likes to take to the broad plains or woods after big American game with some pals and dogs, this is for you. You could live inside and carry your canoes, dead game or a crooked roulette wheel on the roof. It will go anywhere and two feet further than any automobile made in America, with the exception of the four-wheel-drive Jeep. If you get hung up it's light enough for two or three huskies to get it out of Chloe's swamp.

I made my test over my regular route and then took the little apple crate into some rough country to try to hang it up. Zero to 60 runs were silly with this as it is not a high-performance car by any means. I did, however, take it over my skid turns at speed to check roadability and found it held even on my gravel corners. This is a fine road car but if you do get crossed up—and the rear breaks away —get off the gas, unlike regular cars, or you might end up in an early grave. Getting off the gas will bring it back on course, usually. We won't go into the unusual case.

Naturally, like all Volkswagens this is a rear-engine, air-cooled affair. The ride is on the hard side but easily bearable. With a full load it rides better but alone you can count the stripes in the concrete without looking. In pulling power it's no sensational ball of fire. It will climb right up a tree in the first of its four gears but it's a slow process. On my regular hill climb she konked out in second but took it easily in first. As I have already said, I saw these rigs fully-loaded climbing over the toughest passes in the Alps. The secret is to be patient. It will climb anything but not fast. When the grade gets real grim

Uncle Tom and foreign car dealer Jack Penn, who owns the rig, discuss the day's safari in the wilds of New Jersey where Tom tested the Kombi.

Though the esthete may observe that it looks more like a tomb, the Kombi is a rugged all purpose vehicle built for lots of rough work.

Oversize windshields, big wipers and rear-view mirrors give the VW Kombi plenty of visibility from the driver's seat. Top speed is 60 mph.

VOLKSWAGEN KAMPER

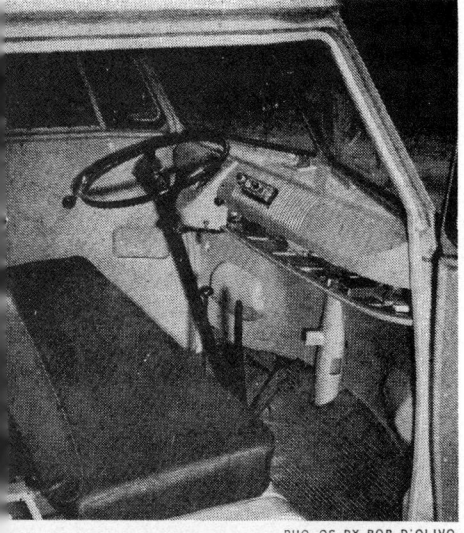

PHOTOS BY BOB D'OLIVO

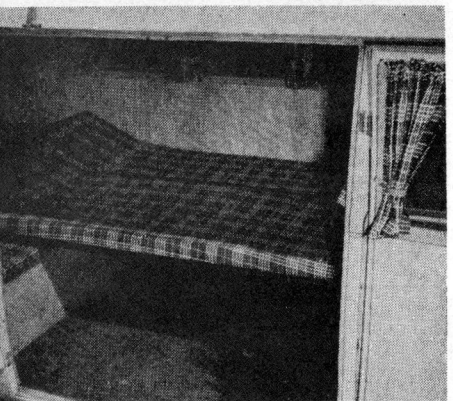

MORE A WAY OF LIFE than just another car, the VW bus, when completely equipped with the ingenious German-made Kamper kit, can open up new vistas of freedom (or escape) from a humdrum life.

Many a car fancier will look down his nose at this bread box on wheels. It makes no attempt to be a high-performance car. Acceleration is unexciting, curves and stops are best taken with all the time in the world, and even a glance at the photos

will show you that the Kamper is top heavy. If you're a vacationer who likes to travel as far and as fast as possible, you'll have to change your habits to be moved much by this car.

Even the ride will demand your tolerance. Tar strips on otherwise smooth roads can induce a tiring 2-step, best countered by letting the right wheels roll on the paved shoulder. Only if you have all the time in the world—an attitude difficult to maintain when re-entering a metropolis with several hundred thousand other drivers on a Sunday evening—will you be tempted. But if you don't want to be dependent on motels, if you like to stop for a day or a week where the trout are biting or the view is straight out of a travel folder, look out! This homely vehicle could make you quit your job, sell your house, or otherwise lose control.

For a *leisurely* trip in a VW Kamper can be a wonderful thing. If the children, or even the adults, tend to get bored, they can always play cards on the folding table, take a nap, or have a snack. All can be accomplished without fuss or muss, tho you'll have to accept the lack of safety belts and the presence of a table that could prove dangerous in a sudden stop. Close the curtains if there's too much glare for your rest; vision is impossible anyway without a side mirror, so you won't be cutting out the driver's view.

When you stop for the night, you'll find that the Kamper's planners did quite a job with a minimum of fanfare. The interior is deceptively simple: just the folding table, a little folding bench beside it on one side and
a plaid-covered, full-length bench with seat and back cushions on the other. At the rear, a hard-looking seat and a cupboard.

But when you go to get dinner, everything is at hand. A camp stove of your favorite type comes out of the engine compartment, where there was more than enough room for it; your camp icebox slides out from under the bed, where there's plenty of space for a portable water tank if you want one. Cutlery is in its own compartment on the big double door,

and there's a wash basin with it. Huge roll-front shelves for groceries make up most of the cupboard.

You may have been leery of using your stove inside the Kamper, but a big transom right over the table dispels your worries. Room inside the car is hard to describe: few people could stand up in it, but seat heights and head room, plus the proximity of necessary equipment, make shifting about both easy and infrequent.

If you want to lounge after your meal, an immense awning with supporting poles comes out of the rear bench. Putting it up is something less than a delight, so you'll probably save this portable porch for your long stays in one spot.

Are the children tired? The front seat cushion, already horizontal instead of slanting to the rear, makes a bed for one of them. A simple support holds the seat back horizontal, too (it's hinged at the top), making double-decker bunks. Unsnap the curtain between front and rear compartments and there won't be any light in their eyes while you read or play honeymoon bridge by the overhead light (we had a Navy surplus light on a long extension, handy for reading in bed when your partner has gone to sleep; but this is not standard).

When you're ready to turn in, the table and seat fold up; the side bench pulls out to become a double bed, cushioned with thin but comfortable foam. Your clothes go in a half-length locker at the rear, on a handy pole, so you won't be bothering with a suitcase. If you do want one, there's space for it under the bed.

Draw the curtains all around, open the rear quarter windows, leave the transom open if you want to lie in bed and look up at the stars. As you doze off (remembering that you got 27 miles per gallon on the day's run) you just might convince yourself that you'd like to live this way, come retirement time. . . .

The Kamper should be compared against car-and-trailer combinations, and in this contest it comes off well. Not only is it infinitely more maneuverable (and not much slower, considering available room) but there's no need for leveling. —**P.M.**

R & T ROAD TEST NO. 119

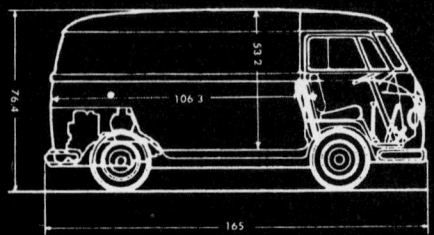

VOLKSWAGEN MICRO BUS

SPECIFICATIONS

List price	$2365
Wheelbase, in.	94.5
Tread, f/r	53.9/53.5
Tire size	6.40-15
Curb weight, lbs.	2430
distribution, %	45/55
Test weight	2800
Engine	flat-4, ohv
Bore & stroke	3.03 x 2.52
Displacement, cu in.	72.7
cu cm.	1192
Compression ratio	6.60
Horsepower	36
peaking speed	3700
equivalent mph	56.6
Torque, ft-lbs.	56
peaking speed	2000
equivalent mph	30.6
Gear ratios, overall	
4th	5.09
3rd	7.62
2nd	11.7
1st	22.3

CALCULATED DATA

Lbs/hp (test wt.)	77.8
Cu ft./ton mile	61.0
Engine revs/mile	3920
Piston travel, ft./mi.	1650
Mph @ 2500 fpm	91.0

PERFORMANCE, Mph

Top speed, avg.	59.0
best run	60.0
3rd (4400)	45
2nd (4500)	30
1st (4500)	16
see chart for shift points	
Mileage range	26/29 mpg

ACCELERATION, Secs.

0-30 mph	9.6
0-40 mph	16.8
0-50 mph	30.6
0-60 mph	75.0
Standing start ¼ mile	27.0

TAPLEY DATA, Lbs/ton

4th	115 @ 32 mph
3rd	180 @ 27 mph
2nd	250 @ 20 mph
1st	340 @ 10 mph
Total drag at 60 mph, 170 lbs.	

SPEEDO ERROR

Indicated	Actual
30 mph	29.0
40 mph	38.0
50 mph	48.1
60 mph	58.2
62.5 mph	60.0

Graph: Mph (corrected) vs SECONDS — VOLKSWAGEN MICRO BUS, Acceleration thru the gears. 1st, 2nd, 3rd, SS¼, 4th, 59. ROAD and TRACK

Swooping "V" with two-tone paint and large emblem gives character to an otherwise squarish front end.

VW MICRO BUS

ROAD TESTING a commercial vehicle may seem more than a little out of R & T's normal province, but the popularity of Volkswagen's compact, utilitarian four-wheelers has risen in this country to a point where we felt an accurate record of their performance abilities would make an interesting report. Also, we have had many requests from our readers who are curious as to the advantages and disadvantages of such a machine as a replacement for a domestic station wagon. Then too, our personal interest in the absolute performance was whetted by the fact that we had purchased a competitive vehicle, primarily on the basis that we were getting more performance. Did we make a wise choice, and if so, what did we get for the extra $500?

Comparisons can best be made by a quick summary according to the following compilation:

List price (VW Camper)	$3150
Top speed 2-way avg.	59.0 mph
Acceleration, 0 to 50 mph	30.6 secs.
Acceleration, SS ¼ mile	27.0 secs.
Mileage range	26/29 mpg.

From this it is easy to see that the VW, in any of various commercial forms, is no fury on wheels. On the other hand it gives reasonable and sensible performance with remarkable economy and utility. Consider, for example, the timed top speed. The most favorable run gave a dead 60.0 actual mph, with the speedometer indicating about 62.5. Any Kombi, Micro Bus, or Camper owner will tell you this figure is absurd—he has indicated 70 mph on a dead level highway for hours at a time. Like the Volkswagen sedan, the larger "bus" is extremely sensitive to almost imperceptible assists by wind and gradient. Our tests are fair, impartial, and accurate, and in this case the odometer read 6900 miles. Tapley readings indicated a good state of tune, and the vehicle felt very brisk even though the figures are not impressive in this modern age of 300 cubic inch production hot-rods.

Like the passenger cars, the VW commercial vehicles have rev limit markings on the speedometer dial: I=10 mph, II=20 mph, III=34 mph and IV=48 mph. The factory provides a warning sign in front of the driver which reads, "The allowable top speed of this vehicle is 50 miles per hour." No one pays much attention to this, or for that matter, the rev limit marks. Factory recommendations correspond to 2860 rpm in 1st, 3000 rpm in 2nd, 3320 rpm in 3rd, and 3270 rpm in 4th. The willing little engine readily exceeds these figures as shown in our data panel and acceleration curve. We used a nominal limit of 4000 rpm during the tests; above that rate the fan protests with a fairly pronounced shriek. The engine is located at the rear, and there is a certain amount of rumble and noise from it, as well as gear whine. Some of these decibils are undoubtedly due to the higher (than the VW sedan) number of engine revolutions required per mile, while possibly the straight-cut 21/15 reduction gears used at each driving

Engine in rear—and a stool is the only answer for comfortable tinkering.

Power for the Volkswagen: flat twin, 4-cycle air-cooled, 37 bhp.

Volkswagen Micro Bus Test

wheel may also be responsible. In any event we did not find the noises too objectionable, even in 200 miles of continuous driving. However, we do recommend that any one contemplating purchase of the Micro Bus as a long-distance travel wagon should drive it and make their own evaluation.

Up in the front seat, which seats 3 comfortably, the ride is certainly on the choppy side, and tricky dips must be anticipated to avoid lumps on the head. Passengers riding between the wheels fare somewhat better, though the seat cushions are quite firm.

The Micro Bus is very easy to drive, has wonderful visibility and easy steering requiring only 3.5 turns lock to lock for a 39 ft. turning circle. The straight-down pedals are a little awkward for an average foot, but the long gear lever gives typical VW shifts, and the nearly vertical steering wheel provides perfect control with a minimum of fatigue (as on our Greyhound buses).

Volkswagen offers 3 bus models, the blue Kombi at $2195, the green Micro-Bus (as tested) at $2365, and the deluxe Micro Bus finished in red and black at slightly more. The middle-priced machine is a very good buy with well finished interiors and good detail work. All three have the unique double-door on the right hand side, and the center and rear seat assemblies can be removed in two minutes. This opens up 170 cu. ft. of space for storage or what-have-you. The deluxe Micro-Bus has extra curved glass panels along the roof and rear quarters, plus a sliding cloth sunshine roof. The Camper has the interior fitted out with 2 bunks, a table and storage cabinets. Floor to roof height is however, only 53.15", and no stove or refrigerator are provided.

As a handy-wagon, any one of the models makes a sensible and economical work-horse, perfectly satisfactory for those who can still shift gears and will be satisfied with a maximum cruising speed of 60 mph. ●

VOLKSWAGEN

Price (Port of Entry New York)
$2127

MOST Americans, aware of the swarm of Volkswagen sedans buzzing about the country, are unaware that the company offers a more amazing package in its transporter line. The four-wheeled flat tops offer a startlingly good combination of maneuverability, space and economy already discovered by many commercial organizations, but overlooked by the average driver.

The transporter models include everything from a flat bed pick-up to a completely outfitted ambulance. Our test vehicle was the Micro Bus.

The Micro Bus has windows all around and more luxurious trim, although the lean upholstery and hard ride remind you that you're driving a vehicle set up for utility not comfort. The seats may be set up to provide space for

as many as eight depending on what portion of the load area you need for cargo or passengers. The center and rear seats fasten firmly to the floor with wing nuts.

A vertically hinged double door on the passenger side and a top-hinged tail gate give plenty of access to the load area. There's a maximum of 170 cubic feet available depending on how you've set up the interior. Some have used it as a camp site on wheels.

The Micro's midget 39-foot turning circle is accentuated by the large diameter steering wheel. Ride is on the chunky side since the driver sits directly above the front wheels. However, passengers enjoy midship comfort. The maximum top speed of 50 mph and low cornering speeds are pretty well determined in advance by the high profile of the body and high center of gravity.

Storming the Alps in a Volkswagen

RUNNING a taxi service over the 8438 ft. Grossglockner Pass, in the Austrian Alps, may sound an unlikely occupation, but I met a driver the other day who does it for his living in the summer months.

Franz Schartner is a wiry little man with the ready smile and charming manners of his people. In the long Austrian winter he uses his "taxi"—a Volkswagen Minibus—to take ski-ing parties to the foot of the ski-runs in the mountains among which he lives. He gives ski-ing instruction to the novices, and what with that and his other taxi work appears to make a tolerably good living.

Strange Device

His Volkswagen is the apple of his eye. Its side panels are decorated with a strange heraldic device, half dragon, half lion, which clutches between its paws an Alpine ice axe. The roof rack is specially equipped to carry skis

I accompanied Franz on his 104th Grossglockner run—a round trip of some 150 miles from his mountain village home. As we

By Our Motoring Correspondent

neared the summit (there were nine of us on board) he pointed to the mileage recorder of his speedometer as it ticked round to 99,000 kilometres—the equivalent of nearly 62,000 miles.

I asked Franz how the Minibus had stood up to it—heavy loads on steep gradients demanding large continuous mileages in second gear.

He told me that apart from having the brakes relined and a top overhaul it had received only routine maintenance. Certainly it was still performing well, even if the shock absorbers seemed to be on their last legs. Despite the large mileage of low gear work he told me he averaged between 29 and 30 m.p.g.

Paying the Toll

It was still early when we started the climb, and a bright, cloudless morning. But traffic was already almost as heavy as on a summer's day on the Yarmouth New Road, despite the discourage-

A ROAD IMPROVEMENT in progress at the summit of the 8430 ft. Grossglockner Pass, in the Austrian Alps.

ment of a toll charge equivalent to between 18s. and £1 for a car and 6s. 6d. for each passenger.

Though the road climbs nearly 6000 feet in twenty miles or so, gradients are never more than about 1 in 8, and present no difficulty to the average motorist. Even motor scooters, with two up and a load of luggage, were taking it in their stride, and the sixteen hairpin bends are wide enough to allow long-distance coaches to negotiate them with comparative ease.

Only when two vehicles meet on the narrower sections of the road does the need arise for a sometimes tricky bit of reversing into the nearest passing bay—a slightly hair-raising experience at points where a mistake means a sheer drop of several hundred feet !

Up and Up

Franz, the expert, took it all in his stride. The Minibus sailed up at a steady 18-20 m.p.h. in second gear. Soon we had left behind the scent of newly-turned hay which wafted in through the sunshine roof, and had entered the cold, clear mountain air in which little but pine trees will flourish. Ahead lay the great snow-covered barrier of which the 12,460 ft.

Grossglockner Mountain is the peak, and beyond were the rugged Dolomites, and beyond, and Italy.

Near the summit, where melting snow was still running off the road, widening was in progress. Huge concrete bastions were being built out over space—a further stage in the achievement of what has been called the greatest road-building feat in Europe.

The Glacier

A few miles further on, after a drop of several hundred feet, we climbed again through cold, bare rocks to the foot of the Pasterze Glacier. An icy wind blew there, and high above a climbing party, roped together, were painfully edging up the ice-bound mountain peak.

A vast car park has been built near the glacier's edge, and before we left it was packed with vehicles of all types, from transcontinental coaches to motor scooters—an incongruous sight in such bleak and rarefied surroundings.

The descent on the other side via Heiligenblut, though less spectacular, is similar in gradient and involves more hairpin bends. We made a fairly rapid descent, again in second gear, to find the charming village of Heiligenblut below basking in a heat-wave.

While the Caravette is a self-contained unit involving no outward alteration to the Micro Bus, additional accommodation can be arranged with the tent extension seen here: it is available in various sizes.

The *DEVON CARAVETTE*

A Holiday Caravan Conversion on a VW Micro Bus

Mk. 10 Calor cylinder from which the supply of the latter comes being housed in a special locker beneath the child's transverse bed at the rear when travelling, or coupled to an outside point when needed for use. Night privacy is provided by curtains on runners to all windows.

De luxe camping rather than complete caravanning is the object of the Devon Caravette: in consequence, no provision has been made for increasing the interior headroom but where additional space is desired a tent extension is available which fits against the side of the body and costs from £18 16s. to £36 15s.

In addition to the standard version, there is also a de luxe Caravette which

THE cult of the motor caravan is indeed growing, for yet another example is now available—the Devon Caravette which is a conversion of a VW Micro Bus. The concern responsible is Lisburne Garage of Babbacombe Road, Torquay.

Costing £897 10s. in standard form, the Caravette provides holiday accommodation for two adults and one or two children but, if used primarily for passenger carrying, up to eight people can be accommodated. The body shell and driving compartment have been left virtually intact and the conversion consists of the installation of a double bed-dinette in the centre of the vehicle, two Formica-covered tables one of which folds and the other slides away when not needed. There is limited cupboard and locker room and cooking facilities consist of a two-burner gas hotplate let in to the top of a corner cupboard.

Although there are no built-in washing facilities, the standard of comfort otherwise should be quite high, for the beds

The main portion of the interior is occupied by the double dinette seen above. The table is Formica covered and, folded, forms the centre section of the double bed which is seen on the right made up. The mattresses are of 4 in. Dunlopillo with loose covers. The rounded cabinet on the right of the door constitutes a small larder and houses the two-burner gas hotplate. Bedding is carried in lockers beneath the seats.

are equipped with 4-in. Dunlopillo mattresses inside detachable covers which can easily be removed for washing, and the general standard of interior joinery, carried out by the Sidmouth cabinet making firm of J. P. White, is of a high order.

Interior lighting is both by electricity from the vehicle battery and by gas, the

costs £1,092 10s. and both models include fresh air, heater and demisters. Also obtainable is a roof rack for £18.

Apart from producing new Caravettes on the lines described, Lisburne Garage are prepared to carry out conversion to privately owned Micro Buses, the cost, providing the basic structure is in good condition, being £200.

Make: VW **Type: Devon Caravette Mk. II**

Makers: Caravan conversion by Lisburne Garage, Babbacombe Road, Torquay, Devon; *based upon Volkswagen Microbus imported by VW Motors Ltd., 32-34 St. John's Wood Road, London, N.W.8.*

Test Data

World copyright reserved; no unauthorized reproduction in whole or in part.

CONDITIONS: Weather : Mild and dry with moderate breeze. (Temperature 46°-50°F., Barometer 22.9—30.0 in. Hg.) Surface : Damp and dry tarred macadam and concrete. Fuel : Intermediate-grade pump petrol (approx. 85-90 Research Method Octane Rating).

INSTRUMENTS
Speedometer at 30 m.p.h.	4% fast
Speedometer at 60 m.p.h.	4% fast
Distance recorder	accurate

WEIGHT
Kerb weight (unladen, but with oil, coolant and fuel for approx. 50 miles) 22½ cwt.
Front/rear distribution of kerb weight 44/56
Weight laden as tested .. .. .. 26 cwt.

MAXIMUM SPEEDS
Flying Quarter Mile
Mean of four opposite runs .. .. 58.2 m.p.h.
Best one-way time equals .. .. 61.2 m.p.h.

"Maximile" Speed (Timed quarter mile after one mile accelerating from rest.)
Mean of four opposite runs .. .. 58.2 m.p.h.
Best one-way time equals .. .. 60.6 m.p.h.

Speed in Gears
Max. speed in 3rd gear .. .. 48 m.p.h.
Max. speed in 2nd gear .. .. 33 m.p.h.
Max. speed in 1st gear .. .. 17 m.p.h.

FUEL CONSUMPTION
43.5 m.p.g. at constant 20 m.p.h. on level
39.0 m.p.g. at constant 30 m.p.h. on level
34.5 m.p.g. at constant 40 m.p.h. on level
28.5 m.p.g. at constant 50 m.p.h. on level

Overall Fuel Consumption for 458 miles, 16.9 gallons, equals 27.1 m.p.g. (10.4 litres/100 km.) (Overall fuel consumption test shortened by distance recorder failure.)

Touring Fuel Consumption (m.p.g. at steady speed midway between 30 m.p.h. and maximum, less 5% allowance for acceleration). 30.5 m.p.g.
Fuel tank capacity (maker's figure) 8.8 gallons, including 1.1 gallon reserve.

STEERING
Turning circle between kerbs :
Left .. .. 34½ feet
Right .. .. 34½ feet
Turns of steering wheel from lock to lock 2½

BRAKES from 30 m.p.h.
0.82g retardation (equivalent to 36½ ft. stopping distance) with 110 lb. pedal pressure
0.72g retardation (equivalent to 42 ft. stopping distance) with 75 lb. pedal pressure
0.54g retardation (equivalent to 56 ft. stopping distance) with 50 lb. pedal pressure
0.20g retardation (equivalent to 150 ft. stopping distance) with 25 lb. pedal pressure

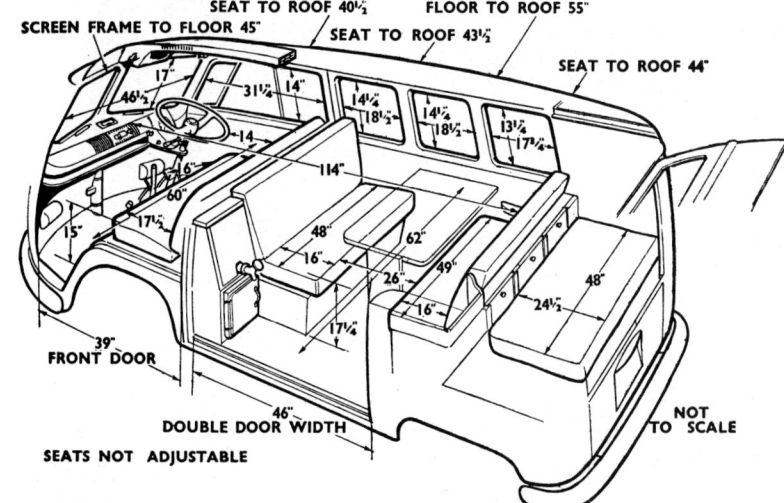

VOLKSWAGEN DEVON CARAVETTE MARK II — SCALE 1:50
OVERALL WIDTH 5'-8"
TRACK:- FRONT 4'-5½" REAR 4'-4½"
GROUND CLEARANCE 9½"
SEAT TO ROOF 40½" — FLOOR TO ROOF 55"
SCREEN FRAME TO FLOOR 45" — SEAT TO ROOF 43½" — SEAT TO ROOF 44"
FRONT DOOR — DOUBLE DOOR WIDTH 46" — SEATS NOT ADJUSTABLE
NOT TO SCALE

ACCELERATION TIMES from standstill
0-30 m.p.h.	9.1 sec.
0-40 m.p.h.	15.5 sec.
0-50 m.p.h.	31.0 sec.
Standing quarter mile	26.5 sec.

ACCELERATION Times on Upper Ratios
	Top gear	3rd gear
10-30 m.p.h.	15.5 sec.	9.6 sec.
20-40 m.p.h.	16.4 sec.	11.9 sec.
30-50 m.p.h.	25.0 sec.	—

HILL CLIMBING at sustained steady speeds
Max. gradient on top gear .. 1 in 16.0 (Tapley 140 lb./ton)
Max. gradient on 3rd gear .. 1 in 9.7 (Tapley 230 lb./ton)
Max. gradient on 2nd gear .. 1 in 6.6 (Tapley 335 lb./ton)

1, Heater air distributor. 2, Headlamp dip switch. 3, Handbrake. 4, Gear lever. 5, Choke control. 6, Heater control. 7, Fuel on/off/reserve cock. 8, Radio controls. 9, Windscreen wipers switch. 10, Body rear light switch. 11, Headlamp high beam warning light. 12, Ignition and starter switch. 13, Lights switch and panel light rheostat. 14, Direction indicator switch. 15, Horn button. 16, Dynamo charge (and cooling system) warning light. 17, Direction indicator warning light. 18, Speedometer and distance recorder. 19, Oil pressure warning light.

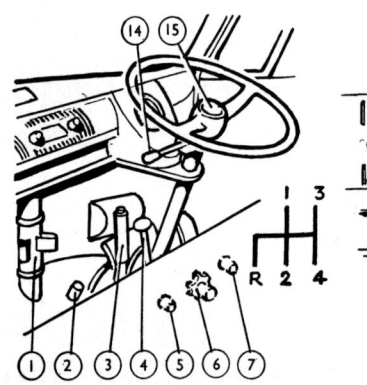

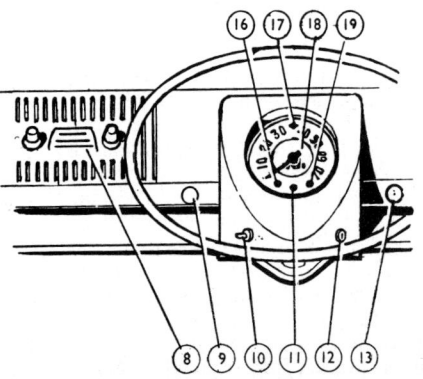

The VW Devon Caravette

A Caravan Conversion Based on the Volkswagen Microbus

The space-saving boxy shape of the VW transporter body, with fully forward control and the engine at the extreme rear leaves a clear central "saloon" for caravan equipment.

MOTOR caravans as a species have merits and demerits in relation to trailer-type caravans which are quite straightforward: given that only limited accommodation is needed, the self-propelled caravan is faster, more manœuvrable, probably more economical, and can be parked on any site which will accept a car; moreover with two up the Caravette restarted on a 1-in-3 gradient. On the debit side, it is less comfortable to sit in or drive than the family car which would ordinarily be used as a tug, and the caravan part necessarily accompanies the driver like Mary's little lamb, whether it is wanted or not. A typical trailer caravanning motorist might have a maximum speed of 75 m.p.h. with the caravan left at home, or 30 m.p.h. (legal) maximum when towing, whereas the motor-caravanner has 60 m.p.h. available every day.

The Devon Caravette produced by Lisburne Garage, of Torquay, comes somewhere about the middle of the price range of these vehicles, a proportion of the cost being accounted for by the duty on the imported Volkswagen Microbus on which it is based, although vehicles of this type are not subject to purchase tax. As a caravan, it offers accommodation,

cooking and washing facilities (but no lavatory) for two adults and two small children, while a tent attachment, which is available as an extra, would help to house more of the eight people who can be transported in it.

As a car, the Caravette's most surprising quality is its compactness. By the standards of private motoring, eight-seater capacity suggests a large and possibly cumbersome vehicle. Such, however, is the saving in space achieved by the rear engine, full-width interior and more particularly the forward-control driving position, that the overall length is approximately 6 in. more than that of a Hillman Minx and the width about the same as that of a Ford Consul. With a turning circle between kerbs of only 34½ ft., it is thus dimensionally quite convenient, and once the driver is accustomed to it the Caravette can even be easier to park in some circumstances than an ordinary car.

Forward control—meaning a driving position ahead of the front wheels—will be strange and possibly daunting at first to the majority of car drivers. In practice few of them will fail to adapt quickly to the "cab" of the Volkswagen. The first impression inevitably is of being very high off the ground, with little in front and a great deal behind. The bench seat is fairly upright and non-adjustable, which is inconvenient from the point of view of

comfort, but less so in regard to control because all the pedals are pushed downwards rather than forwards; the steering wheel on an almost vertical column is also unfamiliar. There, however, the difference ends. The steering is light, but with its big wheel it is not so indirect as to destroy precision, and is in fact more responsive than many orthodox cars, without suffering from road reaction. The absence of a bonnet or front wings to aim by proves to be no handicap at all, partly because the vehicle is naturally straight-running and partly because the height of the driving seat gives a perspective view of the road which is of astonishing usefulness. Far from inching nervously through heavy traffic, a driver sitting above potential obstacles and surveying

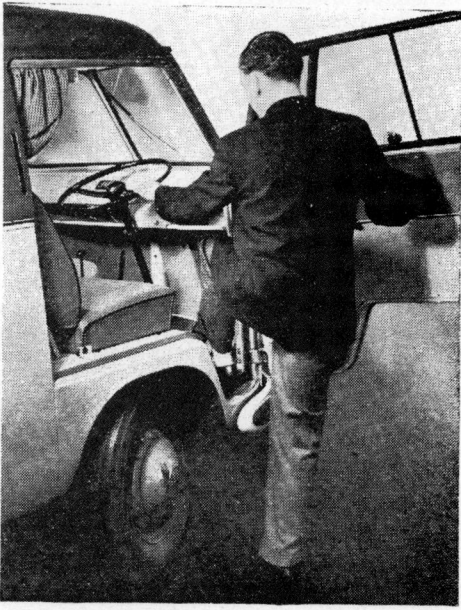

One steps up into the fully forward driving compartment which provides unrestricted forward vision from the non-adjustable bench seat. Near-vertical steering column, slickly positive gearchange and powerful handbrake are notable features.

In Brief

Price, as tested, £930 (No purchase tax)
Capacity .. .. .. 1,192 c.c.
Unladen kerb weight .. 22¼ cwt.
Acceleration :
  20-40 m.p.h. in top gear .. 16.4 sec.
  0-50 m.p.h. through gears 31.0 sec.
Maximum top gear gradient 1 in 16
Maximum speed .. .. 58.2 m.p.h.
"Maximile" speed .. .. 58.2 m.p.h.
Touring fuel consumption .. 30.5 m.p.g.
Gearing : 15.1 m.p.h. in top gear at 1,000 r.p.m. ; 36.0 m.p.h. at 1,000 ft./min. piston speed.

The engine is in a compartment below the small single bunk at the extreme rear and is illuminated at night. This picture shows dipstick access.

Wide double nearside doors open on the interior, which has two wide facing bench seats (a table can be clipped between them), a water tank above a cold-store food cabinet, and a hinged washbasin on the forward door.

The VW Devon Caravette

them over an almost uninterrupted 180° arc of vision, should soon be able to steer through gaps of minimum width with great confidence. An incidental advantage for touring is enjoyment of a view of large parts of the countryside which are concealed from other motorists by hedges and walls.

To revert to steering control, a little practice is necessary to estimate the position of the rear wheels when backing into a kerbside parking place. Three driving mirrors are especially useful as the sliding side windows do not allow the driver to put his head out very easily, but the Caravette shares with station wagons the parking advantage that, although placed rather high up, the rear window is the rearmost part of the vehicle. As supplied for test, the front wheels were fitted with normal Michelin, and the rear with Michelin X wire-reinforced tyres, producing a consistent understeering tendency in contrast to the Volkswagen saloon with which many people are familiar. Although the understeer is not excessive under normal conditions, it can be provoked to the point of front-wheel sliding if a very sudden turn is attempted on a wet road.

Like the steering, the throttle control is smooth and responsive, and 1.2 litres propel 22¼ cwt. through a transmission with an overall ratio equivalent to 15 m.p.h. per 1,000 r.p.m. much more briskly than might have been feared. The air-cooled engine needs the choke for morning starts only after a night frost, and warms up almost instantly. Designed for maximum power at no more than 3,700 r.p.m., it withstands continuous full-throttle driving with no measurable oil consumption, and no apparent adverse effect apart from slight pinking and running-on if straight commercial-grade

fuel is used. A mixture of about half commercial and half premium grades is a satisfactory compromise. The inherent balance of an opposed four-cylinder, and its remoteness from the driving compartment, make the engine reasonably unobtrusive unless it is pressed hard at low speeds in too high a gear.

The rather leisurely performance indicated by the figures recorded with this report is borne out on the road, where drivers given to hurrying must be prepared for, say, a 35 m.p.h. average when they would normally expect 40 to 45 m.p.h. over a longish run. It is, in any case, necessary to make full use of the four-speed gearbox, and every encouragement is given by an excellent central gear change with the Porsche-type, virtually unbeatable, synchromesh on the upper three gears. The seat being fixed, all drivers have to stretch rather far forward to engage first or third, while reverse gear —guarded by a push-down catch—generally presents something of a struggle.

Traction is very good, which could be a considerable advantage for caravanners parking off the road. Soft suspension and the absence of a propeller shaft as a shock-absorber combine to make the transmission rather snatchy under acceleration in the indirect gears, whereas the clutch is definitely in the private-car category for lightness and smoothness. Little need be said about the brakes, except that they appear to be perfectly adequate to the performance of the machine (no opportunity occurred to test the Caravette in mountainous country), and that a full load would probably improve on the best stopping figure, which was taken with the rear wheels just locking. The hand brake is a sensible and powerful affair with a lever on the floor.

Instruments and minor controls for the driver have been kept to a serviceable minimum. The single dial, illuminated at night by a lamp with a rheostat switch, contains a speedometer and distance recorder, with coloured warning lights for oil pressure, generator, headlamp main beam and direction indicators. The latter are of the now rare semaphore type, under the control of a finger-tip switch beneath the steering column which is frequently cancelled from its left-turn position by a long-legged driver raising his knee to operate the clutch. A key-starter is fitted, while there are knobs at the bottom of the seat bulkhead for choke, heater and fuel, the nine-gallon tank including a reserve of just over a gallon.

Caravette comfort has two aspects: mobile and stationary. For the driver and front-seat passenger, forward control magnifies the up and down motion of soft but quite firmly damped springing, and this together with comparatively restricted leg room makes about a couple of hours the longest period for which most people will want to drive without a break. In hot weather ventilation is provided by sliding windows and hinged panels on the front doors, hinged quarter lights and a cold-air intake in the roof which can be ducted to cool either the front or rear compartments, or both. In winter the outside air is efficiently kept at bay except for one or two rather piercing draughts around the pedals and control levers, and counteracted by a good volume of hot air from the engine, delivered also to front or rear at foot level, as well as onto the windscreen for demisting. Under certain wind conditions, fumes from the exhaust tailpipe appear to find their way into the engine bay sufficiently to make the heater

The VW Devon Caravette

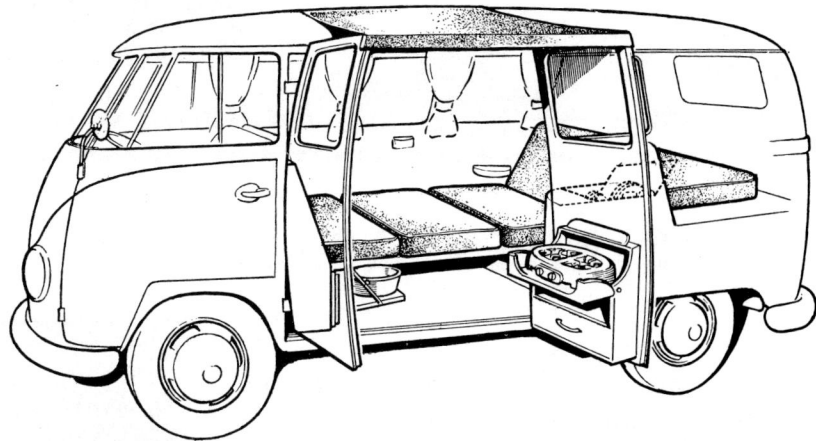

As arranged for sleeping, the seats make up into a double bed supported by the table in the centre. There is a single bunk for a child at the rear and a second child could be accommodated on the driving seat.

unusable by people especially sensitive to carbon monoxide.

For travelling, the accommodation in the main part of the Caravette consists of two wooden seats covered with foam rubber mattresses which, while excellent in bed form, are too thin for heavy passenger comfort and occupy all but about 13 in. of the full width. This extra space is filled by a crockery cupboard and a Calor gas cooker on the right (i.e., rear) of the double-side doors, and on the left by a 4½-gallon water tank beneath which is an Osokool "refrigerator" of the water evaporation type. Ministry of Transport regulations insist that the Calor gas cylinder, carried alongside the engine, should be placed on the ground outside before being coupled by rubber tube to the piping system which feeds the cooker and an interior lamp above it.

The caravan equipment is pleasantly styled and excellently finished, considering its necessarily lightweight construction. A Formica-topped table is normally stowed above the child's bunk which covers the engine compartment; for meals the table fits in the centre of the floor rigidly enough to remain quite steady through all kinds of driving, while for sleeping it fits between the bench seats, when the four tailored mattresses just fill its length to make a double bed. A good deal of locker space is contrived beneath and behind the seats, and in the rear there is a "wardrobe" at the side deep enough for waist-length coats. Beside the water tank is a plastic

basin which can be hinged down into position when the door is open.

A limitation on all current motor caravans is the height of the floor made necessary, if not by a propeller shaft, by the ground clearance of the vehicle in its basic form. In this respect it may be mentioned that the ground clearance of the VW chassis is increased by using reduction gears at each rear wheel. Because of the floor height it is not possible for most adults to stand up, although in fine weather this would be a possibility with the de-luxe version which numbers among its extra amenities a sliding roof. In any case, the limitation is not likely to be regarded as being serious. If one is to predict a market for the

Caravette, it would seem to be divided between commercial travellers in need of a mobile office and an occasional bed, and holiday couples with only one or possibly two children; in either case they would probably pitch camp near to a house or hotel on most occasions, so that there would be no need to live in the vehicle for long periods. For holidaying economically there must be a considerable future for the motor caravan through hire-car companies who can use the characteristics of motor caravans such as this throughout a larger part of the year than can most private motorists.

The World Copyright of this article and illustrations is strictly reserved © Temple Press Limited, 1958.

Specification

Engine

Cylinders	4 horizontally opposed (air cooled)
Bore	77 mm.
Stroke	64 mm.
Cubic capacity	1,192 c.c.
Piston area	28.8 sq. in.
Valves	O.h.v. (pushrods)
Compression ratio	6.6/1
Carburetter	Solex 28 PCI downdraught
Fuel pump	Mechanical
Ignition timing control	Centrifugal
Oil filter	Suction strainer (and oil cooler)
Max. power (gross)	36 b.h.p. at 3,700 r.p.m.
(net)	30 b.h.p. at 3,400 r.p.m.
Piston speed at max. (gross) b.h.p.	1,555 ft./min

Transmission

Clutch	Single dry plate
Top gear (s/m)	5.05
3rd gear (s/m)	7.58
2nd gear (s/m)	11.6
1st gear	22.2
Reverse	28.5
Propeller shaft	None (rear engine)
Final drive	4.4/1 spiral bevel
Top gear m.p.h. at 1,000 r.p.m.	15.1
Top gear m.p.h. at 1,000 ft./min. piston speed	36.0

Chassis

Brakes	Hydraulic (2 l.s. front)
Brake Drum internal diameter	9.05 in.
Friction lining area	96 sq. in.
Suspension:	
Front	Independent by trailing links and laminated torsion bars
Rear	Independent by swinging half axles, trailing radius arms and torsion bars
Shock absorbers	Telescopic double-acting hydraulic
Steering gear	Ross cam and lever, with hydraulic damper
Tyres	6.40-15 (Michelin "X" on rear of test model)

Coachwork and Equipment

Starting handle	Yes
Battery mounting	Alongside rear engine, on right
Jack	Bevel-geared screw pillar jack
Jacking points	4 external sockets under body sides
Standard tool kit:	Fan belt, starting handle, jack, square key, pliers, 2 screwdrivers, 2 box spanners and tommy bar, 1 double-ended spanner
Exterior lights:	2 headlamps with pilot bulbs, 2 tail lamps, stop lamp, number plate lamp.
Number of electrical fuses	6
Direction indicators	Semaphore type, non self-cancelling
Windscreen wipers	Electrical two-blade, non self-parking
Windscreen washers	None
Sun vizors	One
Instruments:	Speedometer with non-decimal, non-trip distance recorder
Warning lights:	Dynamo charge, oil pressure, headlamp main beam, direction indicators

Locks:	
With ignition key	Ignition/starter switch, driver's door, side and rear doors
With other keys	Square key locks engine and fuel filler covers
Glove lockers	None
Map pockets	Two in front doors
Parcel shelves:	Full-width shelf below facia panel
Ashtrays:	One on facia panel, one in rear of body
Cigar lighters	None
Interior lights:	Two in roof (also rheostat-controlled speedometer lighting)
Interior heater:	Warm air from engine cylinders ducted to windscreen and front and rear compartments. Also unheated fresh air intake above windscreen.
Car radio	Optional extra
Upholstery material:	Plastic in driving compartment, fabric in rear compartment
Floor covering	Rubber mat in front, linoleum in rear
Exterior colours standardized:	One two-tone on standard model. Two two-tone on de Luxe model.
Alternative body styles:	Alternative Mark II version of Caravette, and 8-seat VW Microbus

Maintenance

Sump	4.4 pints, S.A.E. 20/20W. (Extreme heat S.A.E. 30; extreme cold, S.A.E. 10.
Gearbox and rear axle unit	4.4 pints, S.A.E. 90 gear oil (below freezing, S.A.E. 80)
Rear hub reduction gears	0.4 pints each of rear axle oil
Steering gear lubricant	S.A.E. 90 gear oil
Cooling system capacity	nil (air cooled)
Chassis lubrication	By grease gun every 1,200 miles to 15 points
Ignition timing	7½° before t.d.c. static
Contact-breaker gap	0.016 in.
Sparking plug type	Bosch W225T1, Beru 225/14u2, Lodge H14 or HN, Champion L7, AC 43L, Autolite AE6 or AER6, or KLG F70
Sparking plug gap	0.024 to 0.027 in.

Valve timing:	Inlet opens 2½° before t.d.c. and closes 37½° after b.d.c.; exhaust opens 37½° before b.d.c. and closes 2½° after t.d.c.
Tappet clearances (cold)	Inlet and exhaust 0.004 in
Front wheel toe-in	0.040 in. unladen (0.080 to 0.200 in. laden)
Camber angle	0° 40' ± 30'
Castor angle	0°
Steering swivel pin inclination	4° 20'
Tyre pressures:	
Front	28 lb
Rear	33 lb
Brake fluid	VW
Battery type and capacity	6 volt, 77 amp. hr.
Miscellaneous:	Fan belt tension of air-cooled engine should be adjusted to allow 0.6 in. sideways deflection under finger pressure. Every 2,400 miles clean engine oil strainer and magnetic drain plugs of transmission.

CARAVANS
Camping & Transportable Boats

(S)MILES AHEAD...

*open country, cities, towns
and villages . . . the Devon Caravette
will take you anywhere, and
your family, and all you need
for a holiday tour with maximum
comfort. Provide your own meals
from the built-in cooker, the dining
room converts simply into a lounge,
and at bedtime, in a few moments
you have a fine double bed with
two single beds for the children.*

in the DEVON CARAVETTE

DUNLOPILLO THROUGHOUT
LOOSE COVERS AND FITTED CURTAINS
GAS COOKER – GAS & ELECTRIC LIGHTING
HEATER AND AIR CONDITIONING
PASSENGER SPACE FOR 6/8 PEOPLE

PRICE COMPLETE
£910 . 0 . 0d
(NO PURCHASE TAX)

THE CARAVETTE IS BUILT BY DEVON CRAFTSMEN · A **VOLKSWAGEN** CONVERSION

designed and produced by | LONDON DISTRIBUTORS

LISBURNE GARAGE | STRATSTONE LTD.
BABBACOMBE RD. · TORQUAY · DEVON Phone 7041 (3 lines) | 40 BERKELEY STREET, LONDON Tel. MAYFAIR 4404

Sole Concessionaires for the VOLKSWAGEN in the United Kingdom

V. W. MOTORS LTD. LORD'S COURT, ST. JOHN'S WOOD RD., LONDON

Volkswagen Pick-up Truck . . .

with the wide open floor

and lockable weather-tight compartment

An open and easily accessible loading floor is essential in many trades — such as building and construction, gardening and landscaping, farming; for plumbers and lumber dealers. Where sides and tailgate must go up or down quickly and easily, the Volkswagen Pick-up is the dream of every operator. It is so easy to drive, handle and load that work is rationalized and turnover speeded.

The most striking feature of the VW Pick-up — unique in this price class — is the existence of two loading floors arranged one above the other. At just the right height, whether you load from your shoulder or from a platform, is the main loading deck. Its strong steel floor has an unobstructed area of 45 sq. ft.; rugged harwood rails guard against load shift and slippage.

Stakes and tarpaulin (optional) can be installed or removed in minutes by a single person.

Below, between the axles, is a weather-tight compartment with a further 20 sq. ft. of floor area. Its lid opens upwards and has positive stay-open stop. Fragile or valuable items can be stowed in this "treasure chest." Of course, this truck has all the famous Volkswagen features . . . the rugged, air-cooled engine, amazingly low operational and maintenance costs, outstanding performance in city traffic or over rough rural roads. Volkswagen gives every truck buyer what he wants and needs most — low purchase price, economical upkeep, trouble-free operating, greater payload ratio, faster loading and delivery, and contented drivers.

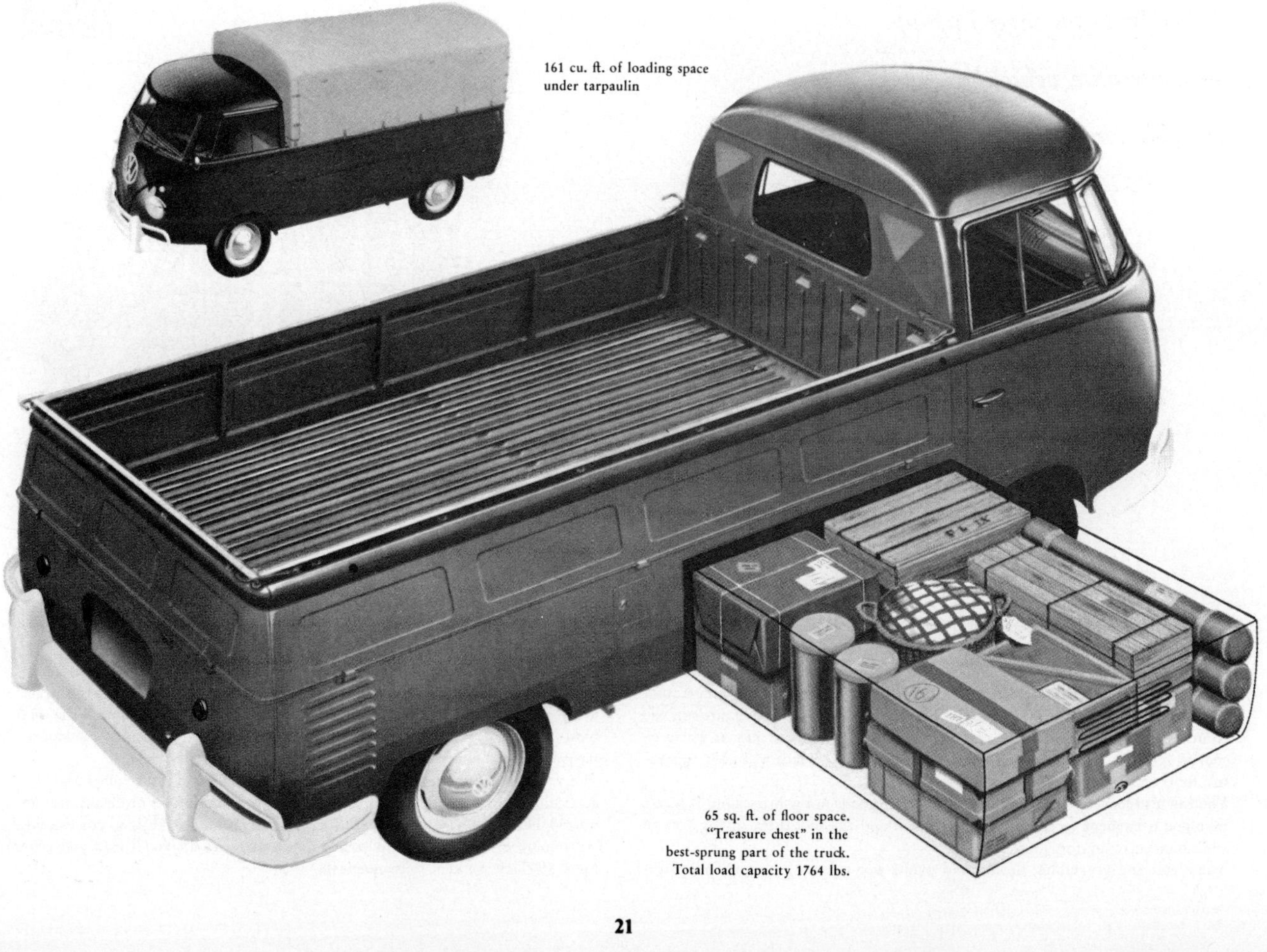

161 cu. ft. of loading space
under tarpaulin

65 sq. ft. of floor space.
"Treasure chest" in the
best-sprung part of the truck.
Total load capacity 1764 lbs.

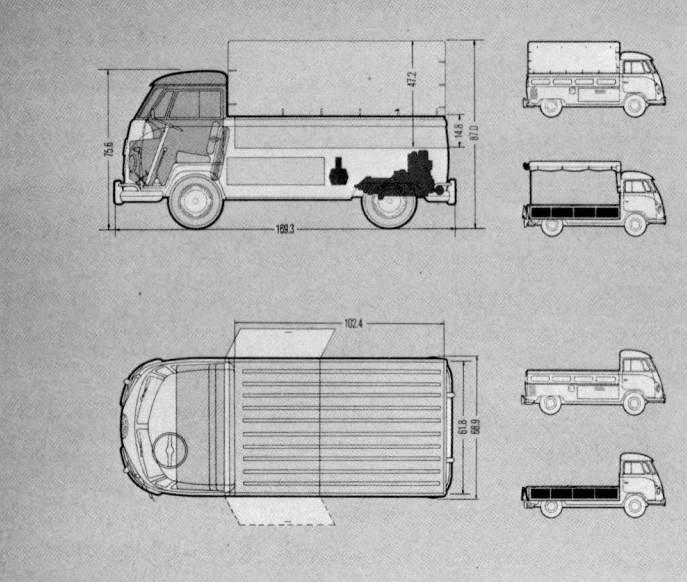

The VW Pick-up Truck is particularly adaptable to different trade requirements. Here are some ideas:

● Glaziers' Pick-up — with one type of pane carrying frame.
● Mobile store and exhibition truck: brings your shop to your customers.
● Pick-up with swiveling extension ladder — for street-lamp servicing, tree trimming, checking overhead cables, bill-posting, fixing neon advertising and many other overhead jobs.
● Pick-up Truck with jinker — for trailing loads: pipes, scaffolding, lumber, masts, boring rods, ladders.

These pictures show just a few of the thousand and one conversions that will meet *your* special needs just the way *you* want. Your dealer will be pleased to advise you.

The VW 6-passenger Pick-up

— a versatile vehicle

suitable for many trades

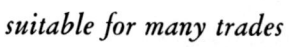

With its flat loading platform and its double cabin it caters for two basically different transport needs. The sides and tailgate of the platform, which is at ramp level, are separately hinged, so it can be loaded easily from all sides in a matter of minutes. There is room for six people in the two cabins, and no temperature troubles either — the standard heating, vent wings and sliding windows in the front, pivoting windows at the rear will keep both the cabins just as warm or cool as you like. Under the rear bench is a built-in chest which will hold apparatus, tools and every possible accessory.

You can also lock away any valuable or delicate goods in the rear cabin. It won't take you a moment to remove the rear bench and the tool chest, giving you an additional enclosed storage space.

Your fruit and vegetables, flowers and plants won't freeze — expensive instru-

ments, equipment, and measuring devices are safe from pilferage. In trades where versatility is a must the VW 6-passenger Pick-up Truck really fills the bill.

It's voted tops by installation, maintenance, building and harvesting squads — in fact by all those who have to take tools, machines and spare parts with them to the job. The right men with the right tools can be right on the spot at the right time — think of the advantages for power and electricity companies, transformer stations, gas and water works.

This vehicle is a boon to civil engineering contractors, road inspection authorities, horticultural firms, and landscape gardeners. No more hitches or delays, no time wasted. Drive a VW 6-passenger Pick-up — it saves time and effort, you can take last minute changes of plan in your stride, and above all you'll find you never knew a vehicle could be so economical.

VOLKSWAGEN-DORMOBILE
debut
ON STAND
86
MOTOR SHOW

Here's another fine Dormobile conversion—a real home on wheels with that sleek, smart Continental look.

See what you get :—

- **Touring for 7** with comfortable face-forward seating for seven.
- **Sleeping for 4** with patented 'Dormatic' seats convert to two 6ft. beds. Also two folding berths.
- **Dining:** Folding table, built-in cooker, sink, water tanks.
- **Headroom:** 8ft. 3in. under elevating fibreglass roof.
- **Storage:** Wardrobe, cupboard, two lockers.
- **Engine:** Air cooled, cannot boil or freeze. Easy starting. Rear mounting means excellent "bite" on all surfaces.
- **Suspension:** Independent all-round for smooth, level ride, better roadholding.
- **Driving:** Car-type all-synchromesh 4-speed gearbox and extra manoeuvrability.
- **Finish:** 3 coats baked enamel for garage-like protection in the open.

PRICE £915 (no P.T.)

Full details and illustrated catalogue from VW Distributors or Dealers, or from

PIONEERS OF THE ALL-PURPOSE VEHICLE

OR

Dept. A, UTILECON WORKS, FOLKESTONE

Folkestone 51844

**VW MOTORS LTD.,
LORD'S COURT,
32-34, ST. JOHN'S WOOD
ROAD, LONDON, N.W.8.**

CUNningham 8000

VOLKSWAGEN

SIX-PASSENGER TRANSPORTER

Germany's latest—a pickup with seats for a family

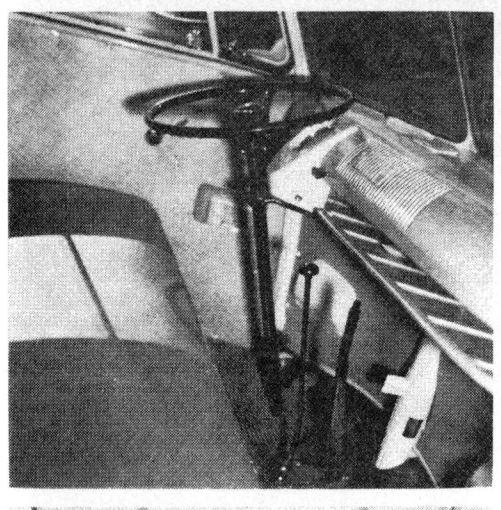

VW TRANSPORTER compares favorably with half-ton pickups, yet its six-foot cargo box can be easily converted to many separate purposes; besides having room for six passingers it also serves as a flatbed or pickup with an optional canvas top.

VOLKSWAGEN'S six-passenger transporter is truly an all-around vehicle. It is a versatile workhorse, an adequate sedan and can provide excellent transportation for nearly any kind of outdoor vacation. The VW handles well, has superior economy and is remarkably well constructed. The transporter's overall design combines the best features of a pickup and a sedan into a vehicle that is successful in total design and in nearly all minor details.

Although handling is good, it is far different than driving a conventional sedan or pickup. First of all the driver sits directly over the front axle and second, the steering is incredibly fast, 2.8 turns lock-to-lock. Visually and mechanically the driver tends to go into corners sooner and sharper than necessary. After a little experience, though, the truck maneuvers exceptionally well, especially in tight spots where the forward position lets the driver see where he is.

The steering is firm but since only 44 per cent of the weight is on the front wheels stiffness is negligible and becomes an advantage once the truck is moving, materially reducing under and over-correction characteristics.

Good cornering is another ability of the transporter although initially most drivers will be cautious for several reasons. The VW is higher than it is wide, in fact, a full 20 inches higher than most sedans. Then with the driver sitting full forward he is well aware of the nearly 12 feet of truck, plus the engine, behind him. In turns this is a strong psychological factor. In practice, however, the transporter has practically no tendency to tip on corners and rear end drift is barely noticeable even in the tightest turns.

Once the transporter's steering and handling characteristics have been mastered, and this is an easy thing to do, the VW is precise and accurate when maneuvering and the driver has a good feel of the road when driving.

The VW is independently suspended on each wheel and this contributes to a smoother ride than found in many pickup trucks. Springing is stiff, however, and the riding qualities are harsh when the vehicle is unloaded.

Entry into the passenger compartment is not good by any standards. The VW sits high and requires a long step from the ground to the floorboard. The seats are plain, covered with durable material and thinly padded. Driver and passengers sit in a straight back position and on long trips this promotes comfort although it seems unnatural at first. Both front and rear seats lack depth, legroom is adequate and headroom generous.

The driver's seat will be comfortable for some, but since it is non-adjustable will be awkward for others. The clutch and brake pedals are too close to the front wall and can be operated only by the ball of the foot making positive control difficult. The steering wheel is in a flat position and even drivers with long arms will have to hunch over to steer. There is no arm rest and the front window slides open only half way making it practically impossible to gain additional support by leaning out the window.

Ventilation, exclusive of partially open windows, is distributed by a duct in the center of the roof and provides fresh air with little draft. The heater is a tube flush against the front wall and near the floorboard. The air, which is warmed by passing over the motor, is not as hot as it could be nor does it circulate through the front area completely, leaving back seat passengers practically unprotected.

Visibility in front is excellent. In the back it is bad. The rear window is small and creates dangerous blind spots on both the right and left. The VW is equipped with only a single mirror on the left side, exterior. Changing lanes in traffic and backing up are mostly a matter of intuition. An interior mirror and another outside mirror on the right side would relieve this situation but not eliminate it entirely.

The space underneath both the front and rear seats is designed to make good use of this often neglected area. Both seats are hinged and lift out of the way without having to be removed. The spare tire is located behind the front seat. Underneath the back seat is a compartment approximately 12 x 33 x 55 inches which will store a large quantity of luggage. When not in use, the canvas top for the pickup bed is stored here.

This careful detail thought extends to the pickup bed. All three sidewalls will drop, converting the truck to a flatbed for wide loads. Each wall is, in effect, a tailgate and can be lowered individually to facilitate loading from any side. The bed is higher than usually found on pickups. In many situations this height will be a marked advantage, less stooping will be necessary to load, overloading will be discouraged and the bed will park almost flush with many loading docks. The bed's 70-inch length may eliminate a pickup camper body but in no way limits the transporter's use as an outdoor car. Optional with the VW transporter is a canvas top that converts the bed into a sportsmanlike camper arrangement and should be as useful as a tent on any outdoor excursion.

With a maximum gross vehicle weight of 4,079 lbs. and payload of 1799 lbs., the VW compares with half-ton pickups.

The engine in this truck is basically the same as in the VW sedan with nearly identical performance specifications. This powerplant is an air-cooled four-cylinder opposed engine mounted behind the rear axle.

Those who are accustomed to top speed ratings which are unrealistic and can be maintained for short distances only might fear the 55-60 mph limit. But this engine is designed to operate for long periods at maximum output and will maintain top speeds without damage.

For a truck the transporter has an amazing economy record and the mpg spread is much greater than in other vehicles. Without a heavy load the VW will rival both foreign sedans and domestic compacts. On a cross country trip with a light load the truck averaged over 25 mpg, in town over 20 mpg. Heavily loaded fuel consumption increases, but since payloads will often be light, the VW will be extremely economical.

Coupled with the engine is a four-speed transmission with a floor-mounted gear lever, synchromeshed on all four speeds. It gets plenty of use, the final gear ratio is actually an overdrive and a good deal of downshifting is necessary.

In true outdoor driving performance the VW will come close to equalling any vehicle but a four-wheel drive. With the added weight on the rear wheels and a high clearance factor it is honestly useful. It will take a 25 per cent grade in low gear and go further down a back trail than most sedans or station wagons.

It is unfair to compare the VW six-passenger transporter individually with a pickup, sedan or four-wheel drive vehicle. Yet this automobile will do nearly everything any of these cars will do and has a personality that is peculiarly singular to itself. •

SPECIFICATIONS

BASIC PRICE: $2330, **ENGINE:** 4-cylinder opposed, **DISPLACEMENT:** 72.740 cubic inches, **BORE & STROKE:** 3.031 x 3.520, **COMPRESSION RATIO:** 6.6-to-1, **HORSEPOWER:** 36 @ 3700 rpm, **HP PER CUBIC INCH:** 0.5, **TEST WEIGHT:** 2280 lbs., **WEIGHT DISTRIBUTION:** 44 per cent on front wheels, **POWER-WEIGHT RATIO:** 63 lbs. per hp, **TRANSMISSION:** 4-speed manual, **REAR AXLE RATIO:** 4.125, **STEERING:** 2.8 turns lock-to-lock, **DIMENSIONS:** length, 168.9 inches width, 68.9 inches, height 75.6 inches, wheelbase, 94.5 inches, tread, front, 53.9 inches, rear, 53.5 inches, **GAS MILEAGE:** 17/25 mpg. **ACCELERATION:** 0-30 mph, 10.8 sec., 0-45 mph, 24.6 sec.

MICROBUS
in East Anglia

WEEKEND WITH THE

VW SLUMBERWAGEN

The European Cars caravan conversion of the Microbus is now available with a Calthorpe elevating roof, shown here raised

FIVE caravan conversions are carried out by various manufacturers on the Volkswagen Microbus van. Among the first to be put on the market was that of European Cars, Ltd., which is now the subject of our first full test of this vehicle in caravan form. It provided efficient transport and comfortable living accommodation through a pleasant weekend spent touring the Fen country, with overnight camping stops in the regions of Newmarket and the Norfolk Broads. It is called the Slumberwagen.

Like the car, from which many of its components are derived, the Volkswagen Microbus van marks a considerable departure from the more usual specification. The 1,192 c.c., horizontally opposed four-cylinder engine is air-cooled, and is mounted in the rear of the vehicle. Suspension is independent all round by torsion bars. Another important difference is that, with the rear-mounted engine occupying much space at the back, access to the interior of the caravan is through a divided side door, instead of through doors at the rear; but there is a tail gate.

Van engines usually share the front compartment with the driver and his passenger, and the noise level is consequently high. With the rear-engined Volkswagen it was expected that the car would be quieter than its competitors, but even then the remarkably low level of noise inside the vehicle came as a surprise. At tickover the engine is scarcely audible, and right through the speed range there is very little noise from it to worry the front occupants. Rear seat passengers hear more, but they are still impressed by the quietness. At any speed there is no indication that the car is being driven too hard, even when the engine is taken up to high revs in indirect gears. Thus the change-up speeds for the three lower gears, marked on the speedometer at 10, 20 and 32 m.p.h., can be and are exceeded without concern, and the top-gear speed for sustained cruising is up to the discretion of the driver to fix at any pace within the potential maximum.

At 23cwt the weight of the Microbus is commendably low and this is the lightest of the motorized caravans we have tested. Although it has by no means the largest engine size its standing start acceleration through the gears is a match for most of them. This is owed, no doubt, not only to the low weight of the vehicle but to the excellent Volkswagen gear box, on which extremely rapid changes may be made. There is synchromesh on all four forward gears, and the ratios themselves are well suited to the engine. In acceleration testing, snatch changes could be made so rapidly that it was not necessary to ease back the accelerator at all, during the split second of clutch depression and gear change; and in normal motoring on undulating or winding roads repeated use of the indirect gears is invited by the positive lightness and precision of the central gear change. Its lever is well placed within easy reach of the driver. The clutch is smooth and light to operate.

Ease of movement is also noticed on the steering, yet the control is amply sensitive for a vehicle of this kind, and there is reasonable response to small movements of the wheel. In a cross wind the Microbus veers appreciably from the chosen course, but it is easily corrected. On corners, the driver is constantly reminded that the engine position places the weight bias on the rear wheels, and the oversteer is particularly marked when the vehicle is unladen. With four people and luggage on board the tendency for the back of the car to swing out on a corner is much less emphasized, though in extreme conditions the steering characteristic remains one of oversteer.

A smooth and very stable ride is provided by the suspension. Road surface irregularities are often felt by the occupants, but there is never any impression of looseness in the suspension, nor any vertical pitching. A fair amount of roll occurs on bends, and in severe cornering at low speeds it is readily possible to lift one of the rear wheels momentarily clear of the road. Off the beaten track in search of camping sites, the firmly controlled resilence of the suspension allows unmade roads to be taken fast, and in soft mud the Microbus struggles along gallantly; severe conditions indeed are required to cause it to bog down.

The brakes are amply powerful for the vehicle's quite lively performance, and the handbrake, with conveniently placed and sturdy control near the gear lever, is entirely dependable.

A fresh-air heater, distributing air warmed by the engine's cooling system, is standard. It proved slow to get under way, but gradually warmed the entire vehicle. It demists the windscreen effectively. There is an outlet below the rear bench seat, in addition to that in the driving compartment, and the locker below the seat soon becomes warmed through, so that it serves excellently as an airing cupboard. Attached to the ceiling of the driving compartment is a fresh-air intake which can be used to feed large quantities of cool air to the front or rear.

Although the Microbus is basically an all-purpose load-carrying van, its standard of finish is outstandingly good, and the door sealing, for example, is first class. It was noted that the caravan fittings were built to the same high standard.

Two large and comfortable bench seats are offset face to face in the middle of the van, with a deep locker against the wall, on their right just below cushion height. Between these seats the table, normally stowed near the roof at the back of the van, can be secured. It fastens rigidly, and once erected there is no danger of the table collapsing. Also, as it has three legs, it can be used outside the van when required.

On the left side of the Microbus, just to the rear of the side door, is a large locker designed to house the cooker. Usually the gas container for the cooker is housed separately, but on this

---

Caravan conversion of the Volkswagen Microbus by European Cars, Ltd. 129, Old Brompton Road, South Kensington, London, S.W.7. Telephone: FREmantle 7711.

PRICES

	£	s	d
Mark I	895	0	0
Mark II de luxe	937	10	0
Mark II de luxe with Calthorpe elevating roof (as tested) ..	1,040	0	0

(Large capacity under-floor water tank and pump, auxiliary tents, and other extras are available to suit individual requirements.)

ACCELERATION

0 to 30 m.p.h.	9·9sec
0 to 40 m.p.h.	16·1sec
0 to 50 m.p.h.	30·7sec
Standing quarter-mile ..	27·9sec
20 to 40 m.p.h. (top gear) ..	15·8sec
30 to 50 m.p.h. (top gear)..	21·8sec

MAXIMUM SPEEDS ON GEARS

	M.p.h.	
Top	54·2 ..	.. (mean)
	57 ..	.. (best)
Third	53 ..	
Second	37 ..	
First	18 ..	

BATTERY
6-volt, 77-ampère hour.

WEIGHT
With full water containers and 5 gals. fuel, 23½cwt (2,639lb).

PETROL CONSUMPTION
Overall, for 521 miles, 24·8 m.p.g.
Normal range: 23–28 m.p.g.

BRAKES (at 30 m.p.h. in neutral)

Pedal load in lb	Retardation	Equiv. stopping distance in ft
50	0·27g	108
75	0·43g	72
100	0·59g	49

HEIGHT
Exterior, roof down, 6ft 7in.
Interior headroom, roof up, 6ft 3in.

caravan a special type of cooker is fitted in which the two rings are part of an assembly built on the gas bottle itself. It has the advantage that in fine weather the cooker unit can be taken outside, but a disadvantage is that there is no grill.

Similarly, the gas lamp is a separate unit with its own gas bottle, and it is held in a wooden container on the right of the vehicle. This is one of the brightest gas lamps we have experienced in these vehicles, and the use of gas instead of electric lamps is forgivable on the Microbus, since its electrical system is 6-volt. A snag was that the glass bowl of the lamp cracked in two places during normal cooling off after use. Subsidiary electric lamps are provided, one above the driving compartment, and another above the cooker with a relay switch on the facia.

Ahead of the forward bench seat, just behind the driving seat, is a full-length wardrobe on the right, and it is matched at the rear of the van by a cupboard on the left side for crockery and cooking equipment. A complete set of crockery (excluding bowls) and cutlery for four people is standard with the Mark II de luxe Slumberwagen. The Mark I is a simplified version.

Sleeping arrangements comprise a large double bed, and two small child's bed set-ups in the front compartment. The backrest of the rear seat folds flat, and the cushion of the front seat mates with it at the same level on a folding wooden platform. The two remaining seat cushions complete the double bed, the forward one being supported on folding legs. In the front compartment the bench seat squab is hinged at the top; it is raised to the horizontal and is then held in that position by chains on each side which attach to hooks above each door. The resulting child's bed, and that provided below it by the seat cushion, is stable, but hard and narrow. A criss-cross of chains at the front is intended to prevent a child from falling out of the top bunk, but there is no such provision on the other side. Softer seats would minimize this danger, and would provide a higher standard of comfort for the front occupants. As it is, the firmness and upright position cause discomfort on long journeys.

Two plastic two-gallon containers, with individual taps, are provided for water. A plastic bowl is contained in a locker attached to the interior of the side door, and the lid of the locker above it is hinged, and is backed by a mirror.

Fuel tank capacity is nearly 9 gallons. This includes a reserve of 1·1 gallons, but as there is no gauge, a larger reserve would be an advantage. The engine runs happily on commercial petrol.

A Calthorpe elevating roof is now available on the Slumberwagen, and was fitted to the test car. One of the best and simplest of its kind, this elevating roof has a large flexible metal panel which folds flat when lowered. The roof is rigid, waterproof and draughtproof whether raised or lowered, and sliding windows for ventilation are included in the side pieces.

This weekend journey in the Microbus left the firm impression that from the driver's point of view on long journeys it is one of the best of the motorized caravans. The caravan conversion makes no pretence to house more than two adults and two children, but this accommodation is provided efficiently, and makes good use of the space available. The construction of the fittings sets a high standard, and careful thought has evidently gone into the design of the conversion.

Above: Ample space is available for four to sit in comfort at the table, of which the mounting is commendably secure. The rear side window on each side is hinged on its leading edge, and opens about six inches

Right: There is no built-in sink, but a plastic bowl is provided, which is housed in this double locker, attached to the rear of the left side-door section. The top lid is backed by a mirror

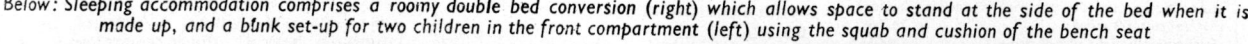

Below: Sleeping accommodation comprises a roomy double bed conversion (right) which allows space to stand at the side of the bed when it is made up, and a bunk set-up for two children in the front compartment (left) using the squab and cushion of the bench seat

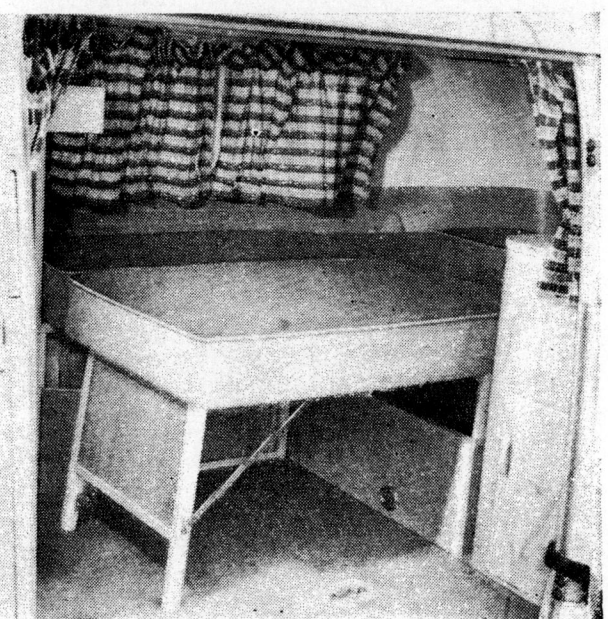

The MOORTOWN Autohome Mk. 2A

A Well-finished VW Conversion from Yorkshire

Entrance to the main compartment is through double opening side doors, one of which carries a cabinet holding the wash-hand basin.

" IT isn't what you do, it's the way that you do it " could well be the theme song of the people who convert motor vans into motor caravans. Take the VW Microbus, for example. There are now no fewer than five concerns engaged in turning this useful vehicle into a mobile flatlet. They all start with the same advantages and limitations yet each contrives to produce a distinctive result.

In the Autohome Mk. 2A conversion carried out by Moortown Motors, Ltd., of Leeds, there is accommodation for two adults and two children living and sleeping, and for six adults just riding. Side entrance doors open into the main compartment where the seating is arranged dinette style and a folding table, which stacks away into a roof locker at the back, can be set between them for meals. At bedtime the table rests between the seats, a loose panel in the bulkhead behind the driver's compartment is removed, and the four-seat upholstery mattresses are laid flat on the platform thus formed. This makes a very comfortable double bed provided you aren't above average height.

With the bed made up, there isn't a great deal of footroom and there is no elevating roof, so dressing and undressing with doors shut is a restricted business that calls for a little practice. Children sleep in the driving cab, where the back of the bench type seat is made to swing up and form a second bunk over the seat cushion; fabric partitions are provided to stop the occupants rolling off. We didn't actually try these bunks but judged they would be quite satisfactory for normal-sized children up to about 12 or 13 years old.

No Toast!

Cooking is done on a two-burner gas hotplate set in the top of a cabinet just inside the forward side door; it can thus be used either from inside or outside. For most purposes this device worked very well, but our addiction to morning toast remained unsatisfied because no griller is fitted. This absence also raises plate-warming problems which were ultimately solved by first using them as saucepan lids. The gas cylinder is carried in a cupboard beneath the hotplate and the cabin also contains a cold storage cupboard and a cutlery drawer.

A plastic washing basin is fitted into the pivoted lid of a locker on the inside of the rearward side door and is swung down to a position under the nozzle of a double-acting, push-pull pump that draws its supply from water porters carried in a cupboard below.

Despite the very limited amount of room at Moortown's disposal, they have contrived remarkably generous storage space. There are good bedding lockers beneath the seats, a small cupboard for boots and shoes, a quite respectable wardrobe (although the peculiarly shaped door which the designer has been forced to adopt does not make clothes storage and removal very easy), and a pair of shelved cupboards in the space over the engine compartment at the rear; these carry, in special racks, crockery sufficient for four people. There is also room on this back section for quite a lot of luggage. All the cupboards are accessible from inside the main compartment and have catches that don't come undone when the 'van is in motion. As casual living quarters, we rated the Autohome fairly highly.

TEST DATA

Makers: Moortown Motors, Ltd., Regent Street, Leeds 2
Based on Volkswagen Microbus

World copyright reserved, no unauthorized reproduction in whole or in part.

CONDITIONS. Dry, gusty cross wind.

INSTRUMENTS

Speedometer at 20 m.p.h.	.. ..	2% fast
Speedometer at 30 m.p.h.	.. ..	accurate
Speedometer at 40 m.p.h.	.. ..	accurate
Distance recorder	.. ..	accurate

WEIGHT

Kerb weight (unladen but with oil, coolant and fuel for approx. 50 miles)	.. ..	23 cwt.
Front/rear weight distribution	..	44/56
Weight laden, as tested..	..	25¾ cwt.

STEERING. Turning circle between kerbs.

Left	.. ..	33 ft. 4 in.
Right	.. ..	35 ft. 6 in.
Turns of steering wheel from lock to lock	.. .. ..	2¾

MAXIMUM SPEEDS

FLYING MILE

Mean of four opposite runs	..	57.3 m.p.h
Best one-way time equals	..	58.9 m.p.h

FUEL CONSUMPTION

43.7 m.p.g. at 30 m.p.h. on level
36.8 m.p.g. at 40 m.p.h. on level
Overall Fuel Consumption for 421 miles, 16.8 gallons equals 25 m.p.g.

ACCELERATION TIMES

0-30 m.p.h.	.. .. ..	9.7 sec.
0-40 m.p.h.	.. .. ..	16.9 sec.
20-40 m.p.h. in top gear	..	23 6 sec

HILL CLIMBING

Time to cover 100 yards from standing start on 1 in 7.8 mean gradient (maximum 1 in 6.25) 14.3 sec.

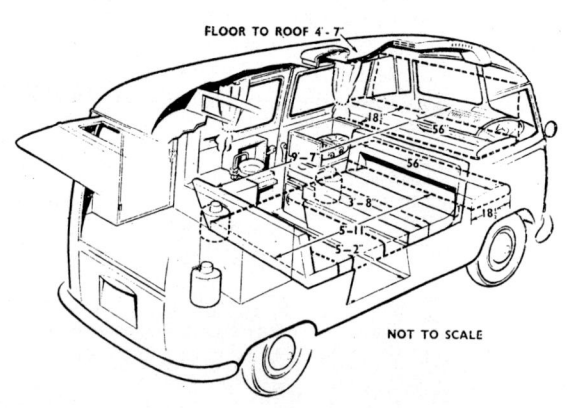

FLOOR TO ROOF 4'-7"

NOT TO SCALE

The MOORTOWN
Autohome Mk. 2A

This general view of the inside shows the dinette layout, the two burner stove and the cold storage cabinet.

slightly less restraint.

With an engine of only 1,192 c.c., giving no more than 28.8 b.h.p. net per ton unladen in Autohome form, a sparkling performance cannot reasonably be expected but it is perfectly adequate for most motoring conditions; moreover, the vehicle can be " rowed along " quite briskly, acceleration-wise, with the aid of the gear lever.

While no detailed braking figures were taken, relatively light pedal pressure was needed to suit the stopping power to the emergency but, on the test vehicle, there was a tendency to pull to the left under hard application.

In forward-control vehicles, driver visibility ahead is always good, and by careful siting of the inside cupboards, Moortown have also managed to provide a fair view astern. No inside rear mirror is fitted and the positioning of the two outside mirrors is such that they are partly obscured by the catch of the hinged, front quarter lights when these are partly open.

The usual good finish of VW products is matched by the quality of the interior furnishings and fittings so, while the Autohome, as tested, costs £982 and is by no means the lowest-priced conversion available, even from Moortown, it will undoubtedly inspire pride of possession in those who care to pay that little extra.

As a means of transport the Microbus is a peculiar combination of car and commercial vehicle. The controls and steering are as light as in any passenger car—a good deal lighter than some—and the gearchange, despite the long linkage to the rearward four-speed gearbox which has synchromesh on all gears, is quick and smooth. But as the front seat is non-adjustable, many people will find the positioning and resultant movement of the pedals, especially the accelerator.

ankle tiring. Indeed, an overall fuel consumption no better than 25 m.p.g., can be attributed in part to the fact that the only comfortable position for the accelerator on any but the shortest run is flat on the floor.

Passenger riding comfort, especially for those in the rear compartment, is good while with a full load the all-wheel, independent suspension settles down to its job better than when the van is lightly laden and corners need be taken with

VOLKSWAGEN

Price (P.O.E. New York)
$2127

THE VOLKSWAGEN Microbus offers more passenger capacity and/or cargo space at a lower price than any other imported wagon. It's a good bet for anybody whose transportation needs alternate from carrying eight or nine passengers to carrying all sorts of bulk cargo, including such items as a Shetland pony.

The Volkswagen has a huge double door on the right (curb) side which makes loading the low, flat floor area easy. The front seat perches up over the wheels and will accommodate three passengers in reasonable comfort. Vision and accessibility of controls are excellent.

The center of the body holds two bench-type seats, each of which is extremely wide and will hold three adults in considerable comfort. Removing the seats is a chore, because they are fastened to the floor with wing nuts.

The rear end of the Microbus is about half-filled with the engine compartment. Above it there is a broad luggage shelf which will hold about half as much—if packed to the roof—as the average U.S. passenger car trunk.

As a cross-country traveller, the Volkswagen has its disadvantages. It is powered with the same engine as the Volkswagen four-passenger car, but in order to carry greater loads the engine has been geared down so that the maximum speed of the Microbus is 50 miles per hour.

True, it will cruise at this speed all day without problems, but considering that this speed may be reduced on grades, it isn't possible to average as high speeds as in other wagons.

However, for those who need high-capacity plus good maneuverability, and aren't planning long trips at high speed, the VW Microbus may well be an ideal solution. ●

3 Station Buses

A N AUTOMOTIVE STYLIST ONCE admitted, half-jokingly, half-seriously, that the most efficient shape for an automobile was the oblong box—it offered more usable interior space for any given amount of exterior. The big switch to station wagons a few years ago seemed to bear out the fact that car buyers appreciated this dividend of space. Station wagons were, after all, little more than squared-off sedans and that large, convertible extra space meant larger and larger loads. But, if station wagons became the style, then style became station wagons. Roof lines dropped, rear overhang grew excessive and sweeps and swoops and fins cluttered up that functional shape; wagons became even more sleek than sedans. Now, fortunately for those who prize utility over baroque decor, there is an entirely new breed of station wagon on our highways and its shape resembles nothing more than that rectangular box.

Volkswagen (which started it all) calls its car a Station Wagon, although it looks more like a delivery van with windows; Chevrolet, basing its design on the proven VW and utilizing its own compact Corvair for components, says its Greenbrier is a Sports Wagon. Ford followed suit with more conventional Falcon parts, labeling its Econoline a Station Bus. Call it what you will, and *we* like the station bus appellation best, they all stem from the same idea and do their job so well we wonder why nobody thought of them sooner. Obviously, there'll soon be more of them on the market.

While the Volkswagen, Greenbrier and Econoline also have the same format, there are enough subtle mechanical and physical differences to give each a different flavor, and, an advantage over the other two in at least one department. For instance, the VW gets the best mileage, the Greenbrier (particularly with the automatic transmission) is the most comfortable, while the Ford is the fastest; each buyer will have to decide which advantage is most important to him.

If you've never driven a vehicle of this sort, you've got an unexpected pleasure coming. True, they're not powerful (40 hp for Volkswagen, 80 for Greenbrier and 85 for Econoline) and acceleration is somewhat tedious. But the first time you cruise down a highway, like a ship captain at the helm, you'll discover that hidden charm. The front seat in all 3 vehicles is high and forward, over and in front of the front wheels. This gives you an uncluttered view of the road (no long hood to sight over) through nearly vertical and only slightly curved glass. Visibility suffers only to the rear but a pair of truck-type vertical mirrors solves this problem nicely. Surprisingly enough, these fugitives from a milk route are just as easy to park as they are to drive—if you've equipped them with mirrors. They're extremely maneuverable, thanks to short (95 in. and less) wheelbases, their nearly horizontal steering wheels and reasonable steering gear ratios; the good visibility lets you "skin" into tight spots. Then, too, these wagon/buses are shorter (see table) overall, than the full-sized wagons, based as they are on compact components. The Econoline, at 168.4 in., is nearly 3.5 ft shorter than the Ford station wagon.

Cargo carrying space is fantastic for a passenger vehicle of this size (any of the 3 have less equivalent volume than the Plymouth Savoy we've also road tested for this issue), but the amount of it is in reverse propor-

Volkswagen leads parade on opposite page, followed by Ford Econoline and Chevy Greenbrier. Below: rear view of chorus line.

tion to the number of seats in use. You can use the buses as vans, with only the front seat installed, or as buses (we gave 9 kids a ride to school in the Greenbrier, just to see if they'd all fit comfortably—they did) with all 3 seats in place. See the data panel chart for comparative figures. Individually, we found:

Volkswagen Station Wagon— Lightest and least powerful of the 3, it also had the best interior appointments and finish, although the Greenbrier's interior was more spectacular. The familiar VW flat 4-cyl air-cooled engine powers the wagon from its behind-the-rear-wheels position and the 72.7 cu in. (1192 cc) are hard-pressed to move the 2310-lb vehicle. An excellent 4-speed manual transmission (our only test bus so equipped) helps it do our quarter mile acceleration test as fast as the Greenbrier with its Powerglide automatic transmission. A welcome feature of the transmission was the synchromesh on all 4 forward gears which meant crunchless shifting into 1st at stops. The 4th gear ratio is 0.89:1 which, with the 4.125 bus differential and 1.4 reduction gear, makes the final drive 5.13:1. Maximum power is at 4000 rpm— about 14, 25, 40 and 60 mph through the gears. Coincidentally, top speed is just at 60 mph, which can be maintained for hours without harm. Long uphill grades, however, can become a bit annoying, although the VW is as

nimble as a chamois on twisty mountain routes. The engine, as with the Greenbrier, isn't very accessible. Checking oil and battery levels is difficult and an old Buick-style square key is necessary to open the engine and fuel hatches. The heating system is virtually ineffectual in standard form. Hot air from the engine cooling fan must travel through long, uninsulated ducts before reaching the driver.

On the other hand, there is an excellent fresh air system overhead which draws its supply from vents just over the windshield, out of the exhaust fume range. The VW has more ground clearance than either of the others, important if you're considering off-the-road travel. The reduction gearing at the wheels raises axle height so that minimum clearance is 9.5 in. We also liked the braking system, which seemed equal to handling even an overloaded vehicle on downhill grades. Our particular delight, however, was the seating arrangement, new with the VW station wagons a year ago. The front seat is divided into 2 separate seats with a walkway between, and a person can walk around the second seat to the rear seat, all while the bus is moving. The Econoline had separate front seats but the engine compartment filled what would have been the walkway.

The VW has the quickest, easiest steering of the group

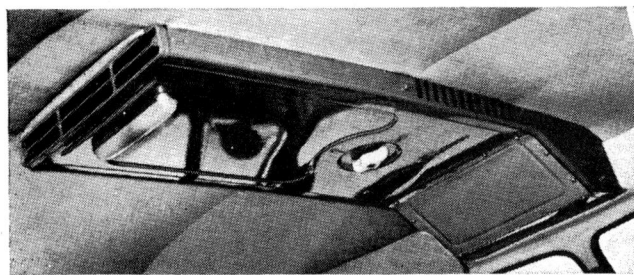

This structure is VW's excellent fresh air system.

Not couch for prostrate middlemen, but Ford's engine hatch. ▶

VW's engine, with vertical fan, is taller than Corvair's.

but it becomes "nervous" in a strong cross wind. If the wind shifts to head-on, then top speed suffers accordingly. Perhaps one of the biggest selling points of the VW is its economy of operation. Our test car averaged just under 20 mpg during all conditions imposed, best of the 3, while claims of 24 mpg by bus owners are not infrequent. Officially, we give it a range of 18-22 mpg in normal operation; what mileage you get is highly dependent upon how heavily you tread the throttle.

Greenbrier Sports Wagon—Capitalizing on the sporting influence of its Corvair series, Chevrolet gaily and wisely decorated its bus with a wide contrasting stripe around its middle—just enough flair to prevent it from looking like a converted bread truck. This, with more nimbleness than you'll find in the Chevy station wagon, almost carries it off. Unfortunately, the engine just doesn't quite have enough push to do the job. The same unit as is installed in the standard Corvair, it puts out 80 bhp at 4400 rpm from 145 cu in. (2377 cc) arranged in 6 flat, air-cooled cyl. As in the case of the VW, this unit is in the rear and drives the rear wheels through swing axles. Front suspension is by unequal length A-arms and coil springs, completing a fully independent suspension. It is this which contributes more than anything to the Greenbrier's really excellent, albeit a bit soft, riding qualities. Handling, too, is good, except in the same cross winds which affect Volkswagens. Steering is reasonably quick and light (no power needed) and the flat wheel position helps even more. Parking and maneuvering the Greenbrier is much easier than one would imagine from looking at its overall bulk.

The Greenbrier is the only one of the 3 which can be equipped with an automatic transmission, and, while we don't particularly like the 2-speed Powerglide (the engine is usually either over-revving or over-lugging), the torque converter helps make it a good combination for about-town traffic driving. It's a little limiting for freeway or highway driving because peak speed in first is 45-48 mph and it takes more than 30 sec to accelerate to 60 mph—we never did quite reach 70, as our test strip doesn't have a long enough run, although we did reach a higher indicated speed on the open highway. Our choice would have been the excellent 4-speed transmission that's optional for the Corvair Monza and we understand the bus can now be ordered with it. Even the 3-speed would have given us better acceleration figures but don't knock the automatic for creep-and-crawl traffic until you've tried it. Our actual gasoline mileage was 16.9, under similar conditions to the VW and Ford—reasonable enough, we suppose, in this day of 12-14 mpg averages for "full-sized" cars.

Interior appointments for the Greenbrier were in keeping with the brilliant red-and-white exterior and upholstery was done in a seemingly durable fabric. Again, 3 seats, although the 3rd one comes as one of the optional extras. No. 1 is immediately adjustable, which in the VW isn't, while Nos. 2 and 3 can be removed to open up the cargo cavern. In addition, seat No. 2 can be reversed so that passengers ride facing backward, facing No. 3's passengers. Dandy for gin rummy games while commuting. We tried riding some distance this way, found it not the least bit uncomfortable or queasy (after all, acceleration isn't going to throw you out of the seat), although leg space becomes a bit entangled. Facing the normal direction, leg room is completely adequate, almost luxurious—something unheard of in a vehicle with only 95-in. wheelbase.

Passengers load from the side, 16 in. from curb to floor level, while driver or co-driver find it considerably more difficult to enter the higher front compartment, 20.5 in. off the ground. The Ford and VW have retractable side steps as options, but it's still difficult for a woman in a tight skirt. The VW solution is best. Enter through the

If these buses had wrap-around windows, nobody could get in. Corvair's cab was among the most attractive.

Ford's interior and ultra-tall windshield is not for people with acrophobia. Note safety wheel, exposed heater.

The New Yorker magazine once advocated the use of VW buses as taxicabs, due to their ease of entry.

"... and leave the driving to us." Interior of Econoline.

Mrs. Smith faces Mrs. Jones in the back of the Greenbrier.

lower side door, walk to the driver's seat via the afore-mentioned passageway.

Econoline Station Bus—The most radical of the 3, yet the most conventional in design, the Ford version suffers a little in convenience and sporty appearance. Falcon components supply the basic mechanicals and they're arranged in the usual position: vertical 6-cyl engine in front followed by 3-speed transmission, driveshaft and rigid rear axle. Where the Falcon has coil-sprung independent front suspension, the Econoline has semi-elliptic leaf springs and an I-beam axle borrowed from some other commercial series. This creates a high floor, although it has the advantage of being flat in the same plane from front to rear. Small (6.50-13) tires, keep it within reach of the ground. Optional, and highly desirable, is the 7.00-13 tire and wheel specification for heavier loads.

The engine, 85 bhp from 144.3 cu in. (2366 cc), peaks at 4200 rpm, which means 25 mph from 1st, 48 mph from 2nd and 70 mph from top. While the Falcon's 3-speed (synchro on the top 2 gears only) transmission is used on the bus, the Falcon's optional Fordomatic isn't available. Even so, the Econoline packs its bulk well enough, doing the quarter-mile and all other acceleration runs better than its 2 competitors. However, the long gap between the 2nd and top ratios could mean you're not going to pass the VW going up that long grade, while the Greenbrier, with torque converter at work, might pass them all. The low 2nd gear is good for easy starts at stoplights, though.

The interior of the Econoline is a little more stark than its 2 rivals and resembles more a converted van than a station wagon. The 3 seats, of which the rear 2 come in various optional packages, are completely conventional with no reversing feature or pass-through to the driver's seat. Seating comfort, pedal and instrument access and visibility all are about the same. Ride in the Econoline is a bit more harsh than in the others and a noticeable front-end "heaviness" caused some uncomfortable jouncing to a lone driver in an unloaded van (the Econoline has some 62% of its weight on its front wheels, while the VW and Greenbrier have an almost exactly reverse bias). We didn't get a chance to run a complete fuel consumption check; however, in view of the Falcon's performance, the Station Bus should get slightly better mileage than the Greenbrier, less than the VW.

We liked the adjustable front seats of the Econoline, although getting into the driver's seat too fast often can lead to a banged knee—from the nearly vertical steering column. We didn't like having the engine alongside us, for, despite a fiberglass hood that somewhat reduced heat and noise, we kept getting a piston-in-the-ribs feeling. At least servicing is simple, and tune-up adjustments could be carried out while under way. This engine location also makes "swapping" easier, something the power fiend will find almost impossible with either the VW or Greenbrier. As for noise levels inside the vehicles, we prefer the rear-mounted engines; indeed, the Greenbrier was the quietest of all to drive with only a pleasant hum emitting from the rear once the engine was warmed up.

In conclusion, we found that each wagon/bus would fill a particular set of needs; if you're interested in one, try them all and find the one that suits your purpose best. Try one, too, if you're thinking about buying a conventional station wagon. There's just something about that high-and-mighty driving position that'll give you a king-of-the-highway feeling even at 50 mph cruising. ∎

Ford, with front engine, is easiest to load from rear. Greenbrier and VW have step-ups over the engine.

SPECIFICATIONS

	CORVAIR	FORD	VW
List price	$2651	$2188	$2245
Price, as tested	3130	2574	2674
Curb weight, lb	3040	2870	2310
Test weight	3560	3230	2650
distribution, %	45.7/54.3	52/48	46.8/53.2
Tire size	7.00-14	7.00-13	6.40-15
Tire capacity, lb	4025	3880	3300
Brake lining area	168	144.4	
Engine type	flat-6, ohv	6 cyl, ohv	flat-4, ohv
Bore & stroke	3.438 x 2.6	3.5 x 2.5	3.03 x 2.52
Displacement, cc	2377	2366	1192
cu in	145	144.3	72.7
Compression ratio	8.0	8.7	7.00
Bhp @ rpm	80 @ 4400	85 @ 4200	40 @ 3900
equivalent mph	85.4	76.4	59.9
Torque, lb-ft	128 @ 2300	134 @ 2000	64 @ 2400
equivalent mph	44.6	36.4	36.9

GEAR RATIOS

	CORVAIR	FORD	VW
4th, overall			5.13
3rd, overall	(2nd) 3.89	4.00	7.62
2nd, overall	(1st) 7.08	7.88	11.9
1st, overall	(1st) 18.4	13.6	21.9

DIMENSIONS

	CORVAIR	FORD	VW
Wheelbase, in	95.0	90.0	94.5
Tread, f and r	58.0/58.0	60.0/60.0	53.9/53.5
Over-all length, in	179.7	168.4	168.5
width	70.0	74.0	68.9
height	68.5	78.5	76.4
equivalent vol, cu ft	499	568	514
Frontal area, sq ft	30.0	36.5	32.0
Ground clearance, in	6.6	7.4	9.4
Steering ratio, o/a	23.0	20.0	n.a.
turns, lock to lock	5.0	4.7	2.7
turning circle, ft	39.3	39.0	39.0
Hip room front	61.4	45.2	55.9
middle	59.6	56.0	61.0
rear	61.6	56.0	61.0
Pedal to seat back	38.5	37.5	33.0
Floor to ground	20.5	22.0	19.6

PERFORMANCE

	CORVAIR	FORD	VW
Top speed (est), mph	70.0	75.0	60.0
best timed run	66.6	72.0	59.0
3rd (mph @ rpm)			46 @ 4450
2nd (mph @ rpm)		46 @ 5000	29 @ 4400
1st (mph @ rpm)	48 @ 4500	24 @ 4500	16 @ 4450

FUEL CONSUMPTION

	CORVAIR	FORD	VW
Normal range, mpg	15/19		18/22

ACCELERATION

	CORVAIR	FORD	VW
0-30 mph, sec	7.6	6.5	8.3
0-40	11.9	9.8	14.1
0-50	19.6	16.2	26.8
0-60	32.2	25.8	
0-70		51.0	
0-80			
0-100			
Standing ¼ mile	25.0	23.3	25.6
speed at end	55.0	58.0	49.0

PULLING POWER

	CORVAIR	FORD	VW
4th, lb/ton @ mph			80 @ 32
3rd	2nd 130 @ 42	165 @ 28	150 @ 27
2nd	1st 385 @ 15	350 @ 26	265 @ 21
Total drag at 60 mph, lb	135	185	n.a.

SPEEDOMETER ERROR

	CORVAIR	FORD	VW
30 mph, actual	27.0	28.8	29.5
60 mph	55.0	57.7	57.8
90 mph			

CALCULATED DATA

	CORVAIR	FORD	VW
Lb/hp (test wt)	44.5	38.0	66.3
Cu ft/ton mile	76.7	90.5	62.2
Mph/1000 rpm	19.4	18.2	15.4
Engine revs/mile	3095	3300	3910
Piston travel, ft/mile	1340	1375	1640
Car Life wear index	41.4	45.4	64.2

CARGO DIMENSIONS
With Back Seats Removed

	length	width	height
Greenbrier	115.5 in.	61.8 in.	53.8 in.
Econoline	84.9	65.0	52.3
Volkswagen	106.7	62.4	55.6

Rear Compartment Only

	length	width	height
Greenbrier	44.9	44.3	39.7
Econoline	25.0	48.3	52.3
Volkswagen	27.6	57.1	31.5

Side Opening

	width	height
Greenbrier	53.5	49.0
Econoline	49.4	47.8
Volkswagen	46.1	47.2

Rear Opening

	width	height
Greenbrier	44.6	36.0
Econoline	49.4	47.8
Volkswagen	35.4	28.7

ACCELERATION & COASTING

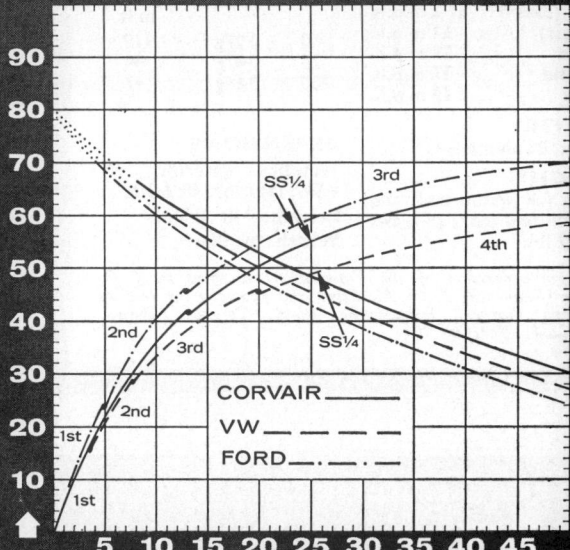

MPH — ELAPSED TIME IN SECONDS

CARAVETTE WEEKEND

ONE of the most popular vehicles for use as a basis for motorized caravan conversion is the Volkswagen Microbus, which offers a higher standard of comfort and finish than do some of the alternative vehicles designed primarily for commercial use.

This test of the Devon Caravette provides our second full assessment of the Microbus and recalls the numerous other good features of this model. As far as the caravan conversion is concerned, the basic design has been in production for some time, but was extensively revised and improved for the last London Motor Show. It is built by J. P. White of Sidmouth, and is distributed by Lisburne Garages.

Rear mounting of the 1,192 c.c. horizontally opposed four-cylinder engine results in a commendably low level of mechanical noise, particularly in the front compartment. Passengers in the caravan section of the vehicle hear rather more of the churnings of the engine, but the noise level even there is relatively mild. Starting is always good, and although the automatic choke tends to cut in when the engine is not completely cold—earlier than

would be the case if the driver had control of the choke—there is no noticeable over-richness. After a night of frost, the Microbus will move away at once without hesitation.

Nearly 12ft separate the forward-mounted floor gear-change from the gearbox, yet the change is exceedingly light and smooth in action. It is adequately precise, and very quick changes can be made. Effective synchromesh on all forward gears allows the lever to be thrust from one position to the next without ever provoking gear crash. Clutch action is similarly light and smooth.

Independent suspension of all wheels applies to the Microbus, as with the VW saloon, and what is probably the most comfortable ride available with any motorized caravan currently on the market is enjoyed. There is little or no float over undulations, and rough surfaces may be taken fast without shaking the vehicle or its contents; although the movements of the suspension are felt, the van remains pleasantly stable and level. Marked oversteer results from the rearward weight distribution, though at 24cwt the Caravette is one of the lighter motorized caravans.

PERFORMANCE AND DATA

PRICES		£	s	d
Devon Caravette (as tested)	... ...	970	0	0
De luxe, with sliding roof	... ...	1,185	0	0
Accessories				
Gentlux elevating roof	... ...	65	0	0
Two-tone exterior finish	... ...	15	0	0
Side sheets and valance for awning	...	19	19	0
Free-standing awning	... ...	39	18	0
Toilet tent	... ...	6	17	6

ACCELERATION

0 to 30 m.p.h. ...	8·6 sec
0 to 40 m.p.h. ...	17·0 sec
0 to 50 m.p.h. ...	29·8 sec
Quarter-mile	26·0 sec

Top gear	
20 to 40 m.p.h.	22·8 sec
30 to 50 m.p.h.	31·6 sec

SPEEDS IN GEARS
(m.p.h.)

Top (mean)	61·2 m.p.h.
(best) ...	63 m.p.h.
Third ...	57 m.p.h.
Second ...	37 m.p.h.
First	19 m.p.h.

BATTERY
6-volt, 85 amp hour.

WEIGHT
With full water tank and half-full fuel tank, 24·1 cwt (2,702 lb).

Caravan conversion of the Volkswagen Microbus by J. P. White (Sidmouth) Ltd. Marketed and provided for test by Lisburne Garage, Babbacombe Road, Torquay, Devon. Telephone: Torquay 7041.

PETROL CONSUMPTION

Overall: 23·8 m.p.g..
Normal range: 22-28 m.p.g.

BRAKES (at 30 m.p.h. in neutral)

Pedal load in lb	Retardation	Equiv. stopping distance in ft
50	0·27g	110
75	0·47g	64
100	0·64g	47

DIMENSIONS

Height: exterior, 6ft 4·5in; interior, 4ft 6·3in.
Length: 14ft 0·5in.
Width: 5ft 8in.

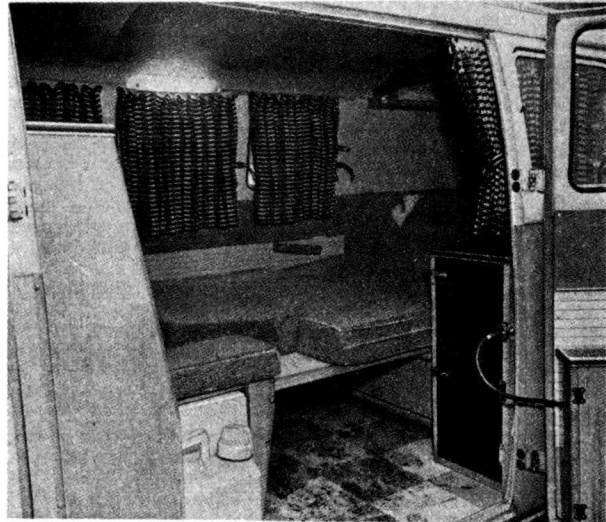

▲ *The main bed is 6ft long, with a mattress of 4in foam rubber cushions which cover the dinette seats by day. The floor is of Polyfloor tiles*

This tail heaviness may also play some part in the pronounced effect which side winds have on the Caravette's directional stability. Light and quite accurate steering allows easy corrections to be made, and when cornering hard the outward movement of the rear of the vehicle is checked readily.

Many motorized caravans tend to be poorly catered for as far as brakes are concerned, but the Volkswagen Microbus is an exception, offering adequately high deceleration figures in return for relatively easy pedal applications. On the road, the brakes give confidence, and feel even more effective than the

◄ *The gas bottle is tucked away in the engine compartment, and has a rubber pipe for connection to an exterior gas point when required*

The lean-to awning is provided ▶ as standard, and zip-on side sheets are available at extra cost. The table shown is used, without its legs, to bridge the gap between the dinette seats when the double bed is made up

The sink (below) is neatly installed to the rear of the caravan, and features a new type of pump with rocking action handle. This was found to be decidedly easier to work than the more usual push-pull water pump ▼

Right: Fitted crockery and cutlery for four are provided. The cooker is ▶ shown in its alternative interior mounting above the fresh water carrier

brake tests show them to be. The handbrake is controlled by a sturdy lever giving ample leverage, and holds the Caravette securely on a steep gradient.

Standard equipment of the vehicle includes a fresh-air ventilator above the driving compartment. During the cold days of the test there was no need to use this fitment, but it does allow a vigorous draught of cool air to be admitted to the front or rear compartments as desired, and would be welcomed in warm weather. The heater is also standard, but was less efficient. It admits air which has been heated in the process of cooling the engine, and takes a long time to become really effective. Delivery at low speeds, as in traffic, is also poor.

Fuel tank capacity is 9 gallons; current models of the Microbus are now fitted with a fuel gauge, and the positive 1·1-gallon reserve provided with the earlier version is discontinued.

Caravan appointments of the Devon Caravette are well-made,

using fittings of sturdy construction, and include all the items —such as built-in sink and water tank, cooker with grill, and adequate lighting—which we consider to be essential in a motorized caravan. Sleeping accommodation is provided for two adults and two children. Facing dinette seats set to the right of the vehicle may be bridged by a fitted wooden platform, which also serves as a second table and normally is stowed in a compartment just below the roof at the rear of the caravan, to form the basis for a full-length double bed by night. The seat and backrest cushions lie together to form the "mattress" in the usual way.

By day, the table attaches to the sidewall and is supported at the other end by a sturdy screw-on leg. Additional legs are provided to allow either this table or the larger platform table to be set up outside the vehicle.

Sleeping accommodation for children is in a transverse bed

Rear child's bunk is installed transversely, and there are two shallow clothes drawers below it

CARAVETTE WEEKEND . . .

which may be left made up during the day, at the extreme rear of the vehicle; a second child may sleep on the transverse bed setup in the driving compartment, with the squab and cushion repositioned in a wide-angle V.

Underneath the forward dinette seat an Easicool cold storage locker for food is built in, working on the water evaporation principle. Additional food storage is provided in a tall locker just behind the driving compartment on the same side as the main caravan doors. Accommodation for bedding is provided beneath both dinette seats, but although good use has been made of the available space, a general shortage of compartments for stowage of small items is noticed.

As a rule, it is intended that the double doors fitted on the left side of the Caravette should be open while cooking is done,

and a side awning is provided as standard equipment. It slides neatly into a long groove attached to the roof above the side doors, and is held in place by two collapsible poles and guys. With the awning in position the side doors may still be opened or closed, and with the right door open flush with the side of the vehicle, the cooker may be folded down, allowing easy cooking in the open. In bad weather, however, it may be preferable to cook inside, and to facilitate this the cooker is arranged to detach from the door and to be repositioned in alternative slots against the tall locker forward of the side doors. When using the cooker in this position, the flexible gas pipe plugs into a second gas tap beside the locker, so that the pipe is not trailing across the door opening. A built-in sink with runaway drain is fitted just to the rear of the doors, and is fed by a rocking action pump, drawing fresh water from an under-floor galvanized tank of 11 gallons capacity. A two-gallon plastic container for drinking water is also provided. Complete crockery and cutlery for four people is standard, and is stowed neatly in a double compartment on the door.

Space shortage is a problem in any caravan, of course, and a snag which arises with the Caravette arrangements is difficulty in opening locker doors and the sink lid when the cooker is in use and the side doors are closed. In fine weather, of course, with the doors open, these problems do not arise.

Fluorescent Lighting

Ample illumination is provided by a fluorescent lamp mounted centrally on the far side from the double doors, and by two additional festoon roof lamps. The curtains cover all windows adequately.

An unusual feature of the Caravette is the gas bottle stowage, which makes use of an empty corner in the engine compartment. A long flexible pipe is pulled out and connected with an exterior point on the rear of the vehicle, and while this system is less convenient than the more normal installations where the gas container is permanently connected, it has definite advantages from the point of view of safety from gas leakage.

As well as for the efficient planning of the interior accommodation, the Caravette scores by its high standard of construction and finish, which is well up to the quality of the Microbus—strictly a de luxe caravan. A Gentlux elevating roof, not fitted to the van tested, is offered as an extra, priced at £65 including fitting charge.

The VW's glass fibre roof panel (fitted with two large windows) is backed with double-coated PVC material. A flashing light on the dash warns the driver against moving off with the roof raised.

The VW Dormobile

A comfortable and economical conversion for touring at home or on the Continent

LIVING comfort for four, travelling comfort for seven and a potential 30 m.p.g. at an all-in price of £915. This is provided by the Martin Walter converted VW Dormobile and, apart from a few minor irritations, all who travelled in this motor caravan were impressed by the well-thought-out design.

DRIVING

The driver sits commandingly high upon a firm and upright bench seat. The steering is light and positive, and the typically VW gear lever is a joy to use, but the brakes need quite a lot of effort when stopping from near maximum speed.

Any driver over 5 ft. 10 in. has to stoop to see through the windscreen, especially on downhill dips. There is little or no sound dampening on this conversion and the back axle whines noisily at anything over 30 m.p.h.

With only two up, the Dormobile is rather tail-happy round corners, but with a full load it is steady and comfortable. Ventilation is excellent for, apart from the usual opening windows, there is a ventilator in the roof which can be controlled by the driver or his passenger, and two hatches in the glass fibre roof canopy.

The window in the back lifts up (when the car is stationary), allowing cooking smells to escape. The two plastic water containers are located here, on a shelf over the engine, strapped to the sides of the body.

SLEEPING

The roof panel is raised by undoing two straps and pushing it up until the telescopic arms click home. This provides 8 ft. 6 in. of headroom and was particularly welcomed by over-six-footers, for nothing is more tiring than having to emulate an ape whilst doing the chores.

The four seats in the cabin will either face forward in two rows or inwards round the table for meals. The seats fold flat into two single berths, or will swing inwards to form a double bed.

Up aloft are two folding bunks, one each side of the roof canopy. These are erected by lifting the inner tube upwards, which automatically opens the outer one and stretches the fabric taut.

At night the cabin is illuminated by a fluorescent strip above the bulkhead, and there is a lamp in the driver's compartment and another (which didn't work) over the cooker.

COOKING

The butane gas cooker beside the sink boiled, fried and grilled, but has no oven and is difficult to regulate for a low gas. The grill is also awkward to light. When cooking, it is necessary to fold the offside rear seats out of the way against the side of the body. The two front seats will also lift up and strap against the bulkhead. Water for cooking and washing is pumped to the sink by a simple plunger.

STOWING

A large upright cupboard to the right of the sink, two more below it with sliding doors, and two at roof level should hold most of the crockery and tinned stores for a holiday. The catches on two of the cupboards are so badly designed that they are almost impossible to open unless prised at their top edge with a finger or knife.

The upright cupboard is inadequate for all the bedding. When not in use, the table stows away behind the driver's seat with the spare wheel.

There is room around the roof edge for odds and ends, and if only two people are sleeping, the empty bunks can also be used. It is advisable not to carry perishables in the space over the engine as this gets very warm.

TRAVELLING

Despite much axle whine and an occasional squeak from the double doors in the side of the car, an eight-sided conversation was maintained on the move. Strong crosswinds on M1 caused considerable changes in course, keeping the driver very busy.

The lights are not very powerful, although they could be set for Continental motoring. Hard driving accounts for the rather high petrol consumption of 26 m.p.g. Driving normally, it should be possible to get 30 m.p.g. Only a pint of oil was added over 1,200 miles.

Much cheaper than a car and caravan, the Martin Walter VW Dormobile is at its best for inexpensive holiday journeys at home or abroad.

VW TEST DATA

Makers: Martin Walter, Ltd., Folkestone.
Based on: Volkswagen.

CONDITIONS. Strong cross wind, cool, wet and dry.

INSTRUMENTS

Speedometer at 20 m.p.h.	..	5% fast
Speedometer at 30 m.p.h.	..	4½% fast
Speedometer at 40 m.p.h.	..	5% fast

WEIGHT

Kerb weight (unladen but with oil, coolant and fuel for approx. 50 miles)	..	23¾ cwt.
Front/rear weight distribution	..	41/59
Weight laden, as tested	..	27½ cwt.

STEERING. Turning circle between kerbs:

Left	..	33 ft.
Right	..	35 ft.
Turns of steering wheel from lock to lock	..	2.8

MAXIMUM SPEEDS

Flying Mile

Mean of four opposite runs	62.1 m.p.h.
Best one-way time equals..	64.0 m.p.h.

FUEL CONSUMPTION

44½ m.p.g. at 30 m.p.h. on level.
39 m.p.g. at 40 m.p.h. on level.
Overall fuel consumption for 1,250 miles, 48.5 gallons equals 26 m.p.g.

ACCELERATION TIMES

0–30 m.p.h.	..	8.3 sec.
0–40 m.p.h.	..	15.8 sec.
20–40 m.p.h. in top gear	..	22.5 sec.

HILL CLIMBING

Time to cover 100 yards from standing start on 1 in 7.8 mean gradient (maximum 1 in 6.25).. 13.7 sec.

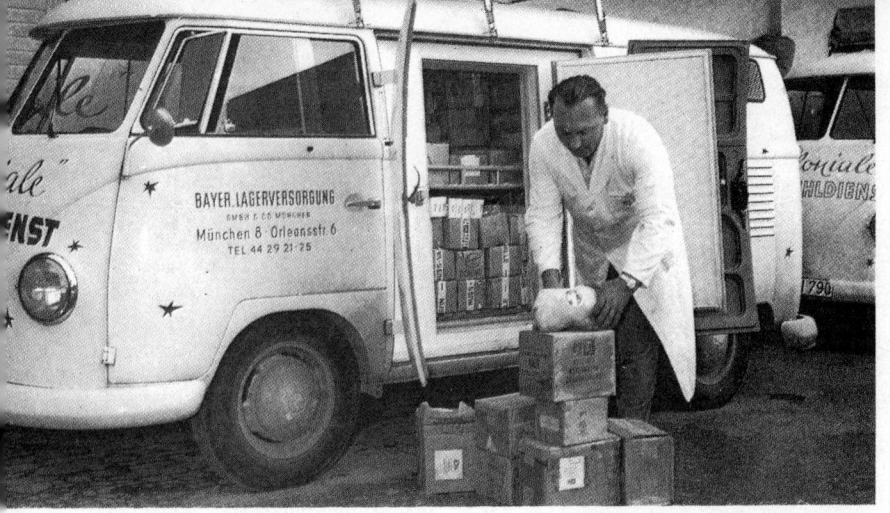

Special Models
Special Bodies
Special Equipment

which have been developed to meet
the requirements of Commercial vehicle
customers in Germany

For all kinds of "high,
. wide and handsome" objects
VW High Roofed Delivery Van ▶

Always fresh and frozen:
when carried in the VW Refrigerator Van
◀ with compressor type refrigerator unit

VW Commercials for every purpose - just the right size -   **80 versions too, well-conceived**

A wide selection comes to the door of your house
VW High Roofed Delivery Van
a Mobile Shop for use in the outskirts
of towns and in country districts ▶

The shop comes to the customer here, too:
◀ The VW Mobile Shop as mobile hot dog stand

for speedy transportation of articles of every description -   **tested hundred thousands**

In good order and ready to hand
loading floor and shelves as additional equipment,
to ensure the optimum use of space available
suitable for a wide range of goods ▶

VW transport

For goods which are sensitive
to changes in temperature:
VW Insulated Van —
◀ protects goods from heat or cold

nd well-made-special vehicles of proven excellence

1 times in practice   -   and praised accordingly

VW COMMERCIALS à la carte

Which type would you like? Here is a "menu" giving you 80 possibilities — from the standard models produced by the factory — to the special models produced in Germany by firms recommended by us.

VW Delivery Van

1	with wing doors on left
2	with wing doors on right
3	with Eberspächer stationary heater
4	with two electric fans in special ventilation system
5	with divided driver's seat and cab rear panel
6	with hardboard interior panelling
7	with retractable step (foot operated) for load compartment
8	with Wido shelf brackets
9	as Mobile Shop and Delivery Van
10	with shelves, counter and folding awning
11	as Display Van
12	as Cinema and Loudspeaker Van
13	as Insulated Van
14	as Refrigerator Van with dry ice blower
15	as Refrigerator Van with compressor refrigerator unit
16	as Mobile Workshop
17	as Fire Truck TSF with German equipment
18	with special fittings for carrying meat etc.
19	with Dry Powder fire extinguishing equipment (825 lbs.)
20	with special fittings for carrying blood plasma
21	with high roof

VW Pick-up

22	with side flap on right
23	with side flap on left
24	with side flaps right and left
25	with enlarged platform
26	with enlarged wooden platform
27	with tarpaulin and bows
28	with two electric fans in special ventilation system
29	without side boards
30	with hydraulic service tower
31	with swivelling extension ladder
32	with hydraulic tipping gear
33	with box body
34	with jinker
35	with box-type jinker
36	with double cab for 6 persons and load area for goods

VW Kombi

37	without seats in passenger compartment
38	with seats in passenger compartment
39	with seats for 7 persons
40	with seats for 9 persons
41	with sliding roof
42	with Eberspächer stationary heater

A flat loading surface offering plenty of space. VW Pick-up with enlarged wooden platform (an all-steel version is supplied, if required)

The VW Pick-up with hydraulic tipping device saves time and makes work easier

VW Pick-up with milking equipment (electrical milking apparatus ◄ for use in meadows)

Upon high — Pick-up with swivelling extension ladder

They ply the roads for commercial enterprises, for various trades, for industry

Upon high once again and this time on a swivel VW Pick-up with hydraulic service tower (Ruthmann-Steiger)

VW Double Cab Pick-up with jinker ◄ (also useful as combined jinker/trailer

43 with two electric fans
in special ventilation system

44 with divided driver's seat
and cab rear panel

45 with partition
and sliding window between cab
and passenger compartment

46 with retractable step (foot operated)
for load or passenger compartment

47 with hardboard interior panelling

48 as workshop

49 with removable camping equipment "Mosaic"

50 as crew truck (Fire fighting)

51 as Police Van
(Accident, traffic training, radar,
special investigation, prisoner transport)

52 as mobile office

53 with special equipment
as emergency ambulance

54 as delivery van with shelves
and special containers

55 with Wido shelf brackets

56 with water purifying equipment

57 as emergency service truck

58 as expedition vehicle

VW Micro Bus (Station Wagon)

59 without centre seat

60 with sliding roof

61 with Eberspächer stationary heater

62 with two electric fans
in special ventilation system

63 with divided driver's seat
and cab rear panel

64 with glass partition between cab
and passenger compartment

65 with retractable step (foot operated)
to passenger compartment

66 without seats as cable repair van

67 without seats
as radiation detection van

68 as camping car with removable
camping equipment (Mosaic)

69 as school bus

70 as control vehicle
for firefighters and authorities

71 with special equipment as mobile bank

VW De Luxe Micro Bus (Station Wagon)

72 with Eberspächer stationary heater

73 with two electric fans
in special ventilation system

74 with divided driver's seat
and cab rear panel

75 with glass partition between cab
and passenger compartment

76 with retractable step (foot operated)
for passenger compartment

77 without sliding roof and windows in roof

VW Ambulance

78 with complete equipment
(German specifications)
which includes 2 stretchers, 1 portable chair,
1 chair with folding back rest
and 1 seat for attendant

79 with emergency trailer

80 **VW Camping Car**

or official bodies, for hotels, travel agencies - used

Formerly this was a VW Pick-up, now modified to the customer's special order. It can be used as a workshop and service vehicle

A Mobile Post Office in Malaya. There's room for a large Post Office Counter in the VW Delivery Van

Volkswagen Kombi, used by the Australian Electricity Trust. The vehicle has a large platform for transporting maintenance equipment. A trapdoor in the roof and platform provides access to the platform from inside

by the Police, the Fire Brigade and Welfare Organisations - What we delivere

VW Pick-up with rear loading platform used in Australia. This was built to the customer's requirements. Loads can be placed on the platform and raised to normal loading height by manual operation of the crank handle

VW Pick-up fitted with glass-carrying rack

Having a Volkswagen on the docks is the idea of the Holmes Stevedoring Co. Ltd., Hamilton (Bermuda). It is for servicing his 22 dockside vehicles with fuel and water. No delays, no hand refuelling necessary any more. The versatile VW Pick-up is the ideal vehicle for this purpose. Formerly these 22 trucks had to be taken out of service for refuelling. Now this VW Pick-up comes to them.

This Volkswagen Transporter can carry up to ten sheep at a time to district shows and stud sales. The farmer uses the vehicle to carry wheat, superphosphate and fuel for farming implements when planting, as well as hauling fencing materials

. . and what the customer did with it

There are many varieties of VW Commercials. This vehicle which is to be seen on the roads of England, has the advantages of a Pick-up. No matter whether the load is carried at shoulder height or rolled up or down the ramp — the Pick-up has just the right height ▶

This vehicle is used in Canada for selling toilet and make up articles to the trades concerned. Not only do the sides of this VW offer good advertising space, but also the very modern equipment which is to be found inside is a good advert, too ◀

FROM KOMBI TO CAMPMOBILE

The Inside Story of VW's Wagons and Trucks

WHAT the Volkswagen line of Kombis, station wagons, utility panels and pick-ups lacks in style and grace, it more than recaptures in function and an incredible use of available space. The box-like VW's were strange sights when they first appeared on U. S. streets a few years ago. Owners who bought them for passenger transportation occasionally found themselves in unusual dilemmas: In some instances parking lot attendants refused them entrance because "we don't park trucks." And often there was insufficient clearance between VW roof and garage opening, a matter determined the first time the new owner put the machine away. But the owners in turn had the last laugh, for it wasn't long until Chevrolet and Ford had issued virtual replicas, only slightly larger than the VW original. The Chevy version, powered with an air-cooled, rear engine, has essentially the same interior configuration as the Volkswagen, while Ford places the engine between and below the driver and passenger.

Even though they are all the same basic size and mechanically identical, the models available can be confusing unless their names and styles are understood. Beginning with the acknowledged commercial vehicles and working through the dual purpose machines into the purely pleasure styles, here is a listing with suggested East Coast p.o.e. retail prices:

		With optional 50 hp engine
Panel Delivery Truck	$1895	$1995
Pick-up Truck	1885	1995
Double Cab Pick-up Truck	2175	2285
Kombi Station Wagon with Seats	2095	2195
Kombi Station Wagon with Seats and Sunroof	2220	2320
Station Wagon	2275	2385
Station Wagon with Sunroof	2399	2509
DeLuxe Station Wagon with Sunroof	2655	2765

The panel truck is just that—no windows except in the rear and on front doors. There is a double side loading door on the right side, which may be had on the driver's side for a few dollars extra. For additional cash it is possible to have the four-by-four-foot double cargo opening on both sides.

A split front seat is an optional extra, as is the swivel front seat.

An unusual type is the pick-up. Its bed sides fold down so that it can be loaded as a flat-bed with 45 square feet of area. The cargo deck has hardwood rails over the steel floor while under the bed is a lockable tool compartment of 23 cubic feet. Extra bows and a tarpaulin (optional) make it a covered van with 161 cubic feet of sheltered space. The double-cab model is a handy device that holds five adults at the sacrifice of 15 square feet of cargo space. There is, however, a tool box beneath the rear seat that may be removed along with the seat, turning the rear compartment into a 65-cubic-foot cargo area.

Unless there is a specific commercial need for one of these versatile (and VW can cite hundreds), the typical consumer is more likely to be interested in one of the several wagons. Many VW fans prefer the Kombi, which is a bare-bones station wagon model with side windows but no interior trim panels or headliner. Some do-it-yourself owners buy it because of its lower cost, adding their own interior trim. But it is most often used as the name implies—as a cargo or delivery truck with the seats removed during working hours, then with full seating for family use. (Seats may be removed in minutes without tools.) As do all the wagons, it has 170 cubic feet of interior space. Load capacity is 1786 pounds or 1643 pounds with center and rear seats installed. Gross weight for all models is 4145 pounds. As the other wagons, it offers a choice of seven- or eight-passenger seating, the former having a smaller center seat for easier access to the rear. The rear door, which swings upward, measures 28.7 inches high by 35.4 wide and opens to a standard above-engine luggage area that is 27.6x57.5x31.5—28 cubic feet.

The ultimate in VW wagon classiness is the sliding sunroof, yet one may have this feature in the Kombi for $125 extra. It offers absolute weather sealing, may be slid open to any position for ventilation and sun. And there are always the oddball utility uses—tall objects that require clear sky above to be hauled.

There are three categories of station wagons. The standard wagon is a development of the Kombi with a hand-

All VW's are fun but some are funnier than others! Design of wagons and trucks may look strange but is extremely functional.

somely trimmed interior and (generally) a two-tone paint job. It has a full headliner, rubber floor mats and sturdy door panels. For another $124, VW adds a sunroof, but the model is otherwise comparable. Top of the line is the De-Luxe, much fancier all around. A sunroof is standard, and there is a series of eight small skylights (four to each side) in the roof adjoining the sunroof. They are tinted, admit light, permit passengers to see overhead scenery, generally add to the vehicle's charm. The DeLuxe model includes such other goodies as an electric clock, padded sun visors, chrome door fittings, assist strap and three clothes hooks in the passenger compartment, a carpeted luggage section, tie-down rails to protect the windows in the luggage area, rubber bumper moldings and extra chrome trim around the waistline and on the engine air intake louvers. Interestingly enough, the DeLuxe may be ordered without sunroof or skylights.

Admittedly a box on wheels, the wagon appears to be much longer than it is. At 168.9 inches overall (pick-ups and the DeLuxe are 169.3), it is only 8.9 inches longer than the standard sedan. Ease of parking and startling maneuverability within a 39-foot turning circle follows naturally.

Wheelbase is 94.5 inches, front tread 54.2, rear tread 53.5, and overall width is 68.9 inches.

Unless the novice station wagon driver has had some experience with cab-over-engine trucks, driving VW's rolling platform is a brand-new sensation that requires some getting used to. For one thing, the driver is only the thickness of the front body steel from other traffic and at first there is this gnawing awareness that he is going to hit something. Without an engine or hood out front it is possible to come alarmingly close to other cars and not touch. It especially makes parking an interesting experience the first few times. The driver is seated directly over the front wheels and his feet are actually ahead of them so that the feeling is quite unlike parking a conventional car. Not difficult, but different. Because of the high rear window, parking and backing are best undertaken with the aid of carefully adjusted side mirrors. The view to the rear is at such an elevation that it is possible to back right into a low sports car, the tinkle of broken headlights and smashed grille being the first warning of anything amiss.

Cockpit room is ample and the driver's seat is adjustable. The steering wheel is nearly horizontal, much like a bus, and

provides quite a pleasing position after one becomes accustomed to it.

There is 9.4 inches of road clearance through the entire line of wagons and trucks. This is dandy for pulling deeply rutted trails without hanging up, and it was necessary in the design to prevent the wheels from infringing into the vehicle more than they do. But when this road clearance is considered with the 76.4 inches overall height, it reveals a tall, slightly top heavy car. In practical terms, it means that, unlike most modern autos, it is possible to tip a station wagon by cornering too fast. There is no pressing danger, but it has happened, mostly through carelessness, failing to observe posted curve limits, that sort of thing.

Experienced station wagon drivers generally concede that the VW's rated top speed of 65 mph (also its cruising) with the 1500 engine is about the maximum safe velocity. It is entirely possible to see considerably more speed on a downhill run, but a sudden change of direction could be disastrous. Making the speed factor even more significant are the many wagons on the streets with various power combinations —hopped up VW engines, Porsche power, and a few with Corvair mills—all of which make the car capable of very high speeds. The smart pilots use the extra horses to help them up hills at comfortable speeds or for added acceleration, not for top end speed.

The road clearance, incidentally, makes that first step into the front seat a high one. A girl with a tight skirt will find it embarrassingly difficult to retain much modesty if she is faced with the problem of entering the driver's seat. And alighting can be equally interesting. Most women simply avoid such clothes when driving the wagon. A useful spring-loaded retractable step is optional at the side doors, and is a great convenience for rear seat passengers.

The standard wagon and truck engine is VW's faithful 72.7-cubic-inch, 40-hp unit, the same flat-four that has been in the passenger car for many years. However, the price listing carries an optional 50-hp engine, about $100-110 extra, and the fact is that beginning in 1963, almost all the wagons imported to the U. S. had this powerplant. It is the 1500 engine (91.9 cubic inches) that powers the VW 1500. While it has substantial differences from the older model, the primary one with which we are concerned is its increased power, something that the wagon had needed since its introduction.

With the early engine, top speed was about 60 mph, and it was not uncommon to have to pull even modest grades in third gear, flat out at about 35 mph with only a medium load. Granted, that the enforced speed reduction often came

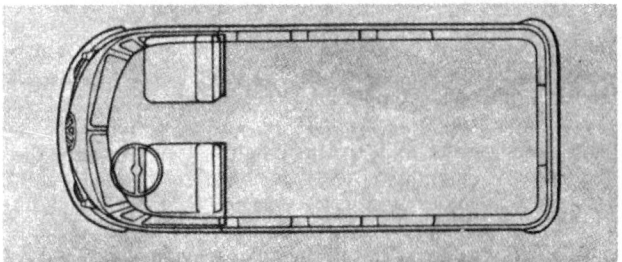
Two-passenger Kombi setup employs pair of front bucket seats.

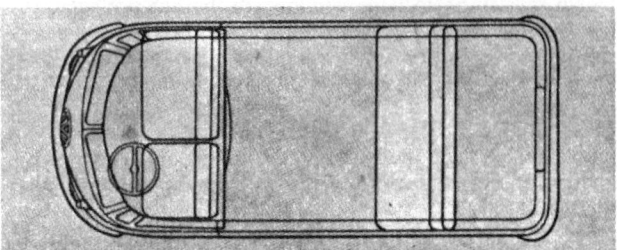
Arranged for five people, Kombi allows plenty of rear legroom!

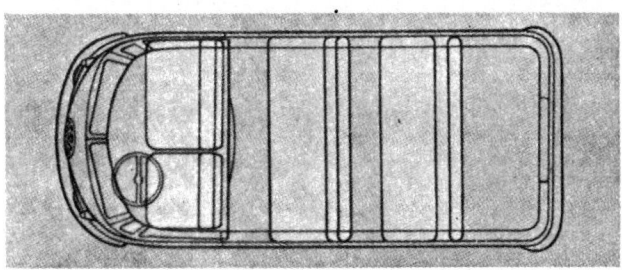
Maximum Kombi seating is designed to accommodate eight.

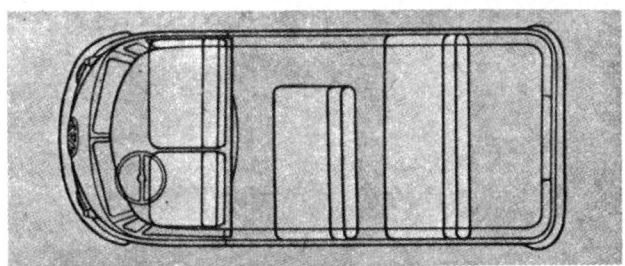
Seven-place seating allows easier access to rear compartment.

Top—Kombi, VW's most utilitarian wagon model, accommodates eight adult passengers or as much as 1786 lbs. cargo.

Above—Wide double doors on curb side provide opening nearly four feet square. Interior of vehicle has 170 cu. ft. of space.

Left—Low-priced Kombi is distinguished from other VW wagons by its spartan look. Interior lacks trim panels, headliner.

as a welcome period of relaxation during a long trip, but it was likewise frustrating to see domestic autos zipping past at 65. The added power has not completely solved the problem, but it has been alleviated.

Wagons with the small engine have a final drive ratio of 5.73:1, quite a limiting factor for speed, but a veritable stump puller in the lower gears. With the larger engine, the ratio has been reduced to 5.21:1, one reason for the additional speed rating. Top transmission gear in the VW wagon is an overdrive, .82:1, and the final drive is actually accomplished by spur reduction gears at the rear wheels.

The wagons have never been much on acceleration through

"Standard" wagon, despite the nomenclature, is cut above Kombi, features two-tone paint and fully-trimmed interior, including rubber floor mats and sturdy door panels. Length of vehicle is 168.9 inches, 8.9 inches more than 1200 sedan. Result is remarkable space within easy-to-maneuver dimensions.

the gears, although they are adequate to keep up with normal traffic. Early models had warning segments on the speedo, indicating shift points for each gear. It was a fairly common practice for drivers in a hurry to rev the engine so high that they shifted at or very near the mark for the next highest gear. It is probably a tribute to the car's amazing durability that the engine seldom gave any protest.

As a matter of interest, the fuel induction and exhaust system is designed with such a lack of breathing ability that it is difficult to over-rev the engine and do it any damage, except for a possible accidental downshift at high speed. The engine develops its 50 hp at 3900 rpm, at which point the piston speed is a very low and safe 1768 feet per minute.

Rated fuel consumption on the wagon is 24 mpg, arrived at by taking actual consumption plus 10 per cent with half payload at a steady ¾ of the 65-mph top speed on a level road. This typical German thoroughness gives a figure that is not unreasonable in everyday use. The factory rates climbing ability (a point rarely revealed about U. S. vehicles) fully loaded at a 28 per cent grade in first gear, 14.5 per cent in second, 7.5 per cent in third, and four per cent in high. What this indicates is that there are very few hills that will faze the VW—even when loaded to the gunwales.

Brakes have always been just adequate on Volkswagens. The wagons with 1500 engines have 159 square inches of lining area as compared to 130 square inches on the standard-engined wagon. They do a satisfactory job and it would be only the extreme condition—fully loaded down a steep mountain grade—where significant fade might be encountered. In such an event it would be hoped that the driver would be descending in a low gear to help compensate.

The truck and wagon suspension is basically the same design as in the sedan—all wheels independent via transverse torsion bars and tubular shocks. As a consequence, the ride is good, far better than one would suppose from such a utilitarian vehicle. As long as the generous load limits are not surpassed there is no need for any sort of overload springing. In fact, it would be difficult to figure out any means of adding it, except for heavier shocks or possibly an extra set all around.

As on the passenger car, the heating system is standard and does a reasonable job except in the very coldest of climates where there have been heard complaints that it is tough to heat the interior adequately. Non-factory auxiliary heaters are available and work well. When opened, the interior venting system delivers a steady supply of fresh air

DeLuxe station wagon has even fancier paint work, extra glass area for better visibility to the rear and higher-quality finish inside. Special bumpers put its length up to 169.3 inches. All VW wagons and trucks come with familiar 1200 engine as standard equipment; 1500 unit is optional at $110 extra.

from a vent above the windshield that ducts air into the cab roof. It can be assisted by an optional electric fan, not exactly air conditioning, but it keeps the air circulating.

Volkswagen, of course, makes a strong case for overall operating economy. They claim that costs should run about 2.5 cents per mile, about half what it costs most light trucks. As for service, factory-trained mechanics are supposed to be able to remove and replace an engine in 90 minutes. Stressing inexpensive parts, VW quotes $9.95 for a new fuel

pump, a cylinder with piston and rings at $17.14, and a whole rear quarter panel for the DeLuxe wagon at $43.85— all plus installation, but indicative of nominal maintenance costs.

With the sensational boom in motorized campers, installed on almost anything that is self-powered, it stands to reason that VW would have such equipment. In fact, they were among the first. A handful of attractive campers, fitted out in Germany, made their appearance some years ago in VW

Fancy extras, such as sunroof and eight small skylight windows, available throughout wagon line but are thought of in connection with DeLuxe version. Result is luxurious vehicle.

dealerships. They had price tags of slightly more than $3000 and some even had a special roof panel that could be elevated for stand-up headroom. Thriftier owners made their own conversions to suit their needs, and now a series of six Campmobile kits are available to be fitted to existing panels, Kombis and wagons.

The T-500 kit is one of the most interesting because it is designed for the panel truck. Listing at $530, it consists of five gear-operated and screened safety glass windows, small but adequate for light and air when they are installed in the solid body sides. Additionally, there is complete ceiling and side-wall birch paneling; seats which unfold to form a double bed; vinyl floor covering; folding table with extension leaf; two side-door shelves; clothes closet with mirror on door;

Panel truck is based on same body shell as wagon but doesn't have side windows. Payload is also slightly higher, 1830 lbs. against 1786 for wagon. Options include swivel seat for driver.

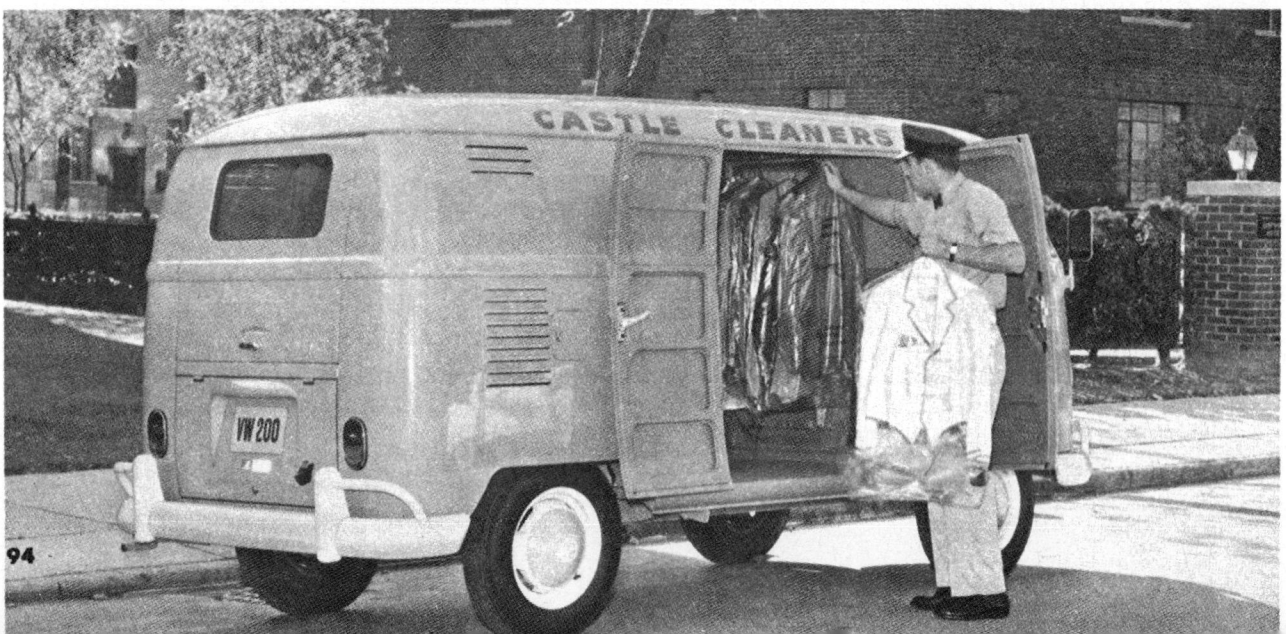

Forward cab design of VW trucks proved especially useful feature on pickup, allows bed 102.4 inches long and 61.8 inches wide for total area of 45 square feet. Payload is 1764 lbs.

two wall-mounted electric lamps; six foam rubber cushions covered with vinyl or nylon fabric; food storage compartment; soil resistant window curtains; magazine cabinet; three floor-level storage cabinets with drop doors; and a hidden storage compartment behind the driver's seat.

A deluxe kit for the panel truck is the T-400, priced at $730. It is the same as the T-500, but it adds a cabinet housing, a 50-pound ice box and 14-gallon water storage tank with chrome pump and swivel spigot; a two-burner gas stove; and a chemical toilet.

The T-700 kit is for the VW station wagon and is identical to the T-500 (the first one listed) except that it is without side windows and interior paneling which are standard equipment on the wagons. The suggested retail list price is $465.

Moving along through the numbers, the T-600 is the deluxe kit for station wagons, and it matches the T-400, less side windows and interior paneling, unneeded for wagons, at $570.

There are two kits for Kombis. The T-900 is $465, is the same as the T-500 less side windows. Finally, the T-800, the deluxe kit, is identical to the T-400 less side windows. Price: $690.

There is a list of optional accessories for the Campmobile

Double-cab pickup holds five passengers plus 1058 lbs. of cargo. Bed measures 30 square feet. Both pickups feature sides that drop like tailgates, converting to easily-loaded flat beds.

kits that will permit the prospective outdoorsman to rough it in even greater comfort. A roll-up awning tent (and roof carrier) providing a six-by-six-foot enclosed "room" is $88, while a free-standing eight-by-eight-foot cabana tent with roof carrier goes for $125. People, it seems, are accustomed to washing all over and hate to give it up away from home, hence the popularity of a 25-gallon shower unit and fittings ($46.50), and a canvas shower enclosure ($16.34).

Sun worshipers can have a sun deck and access ladder, using the deck for luggage while in transit, for $104.50. For extra sleeping room, there is the Campette at $87.60, a roof-mounted pack which is cleverly designed to open into a mosquito- and weather-proof double bedroom. A set of four mattresses for the Campette is $48. Sleepwalkers or sufferers from acrophobia would probably not find it very restful. For more sleeping, there is a hammock sling that installs above the front seat, suitable for one child, $10.

A luggage rack cover ($22), and four sliding window screens for the Kombi or wagon ($29) round out the list of accessories for outdoor lovers.

In spite of a few disbelievers who can't quite see why anyone would actually want to ride around in one of those funny looking things, there seems no doubt that the VW wagon is here to stay. The boldly practical concept is just too good to pass by. Apparently, then, the only thing between the VW and total public acceptance is the attitude of misinformed parking lot attendants. Or are they misinformed? After all, some of them are trucks, aren't they? ■

Ultimate in outdoor comfort is Campmobile, conversion involving any of six kits that can be adapted to any VW Kombi, wagon or panel truck. Campmobile accessories include special furnishings such as gas stove, water storage tank, portable shower and chemical toilet. Variety of tents are available.

1964 Volkswagens on Parade

VW-1261-64

VW-1266-64

VW-1275-64

VW-1253-64

VW-1270-64

VW-1273-64

Devon Caravette with awning erected. Side curtains can be added to make an extra "room" for preparing meals.

Without the optional extending roof, the Volkswagen is very compact. Though interior headroom is a little restricted in practice this was not found to be a problem.

4' 8"
6' 4"
5' 9"

The Devon Caravette

" . . . a comfortable, long-legged and economical family tourer . . ."

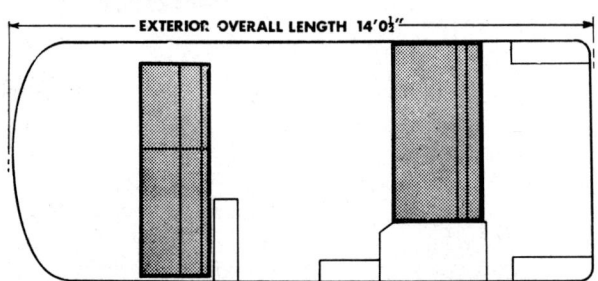

EXTERIOR OVERALL LENGTH 14' 0½"

Driving   The driver's seat is adjustable; there are places for four passengers facing forward.

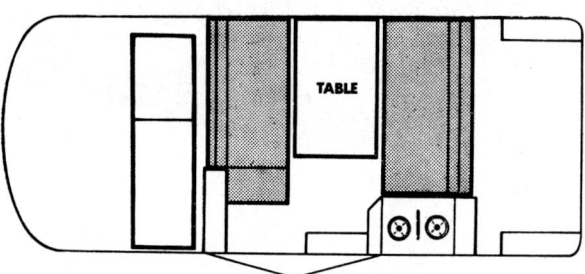

TABLE

Eating   Four sit round the table. The cooker can be fitted on the right-hand side door.

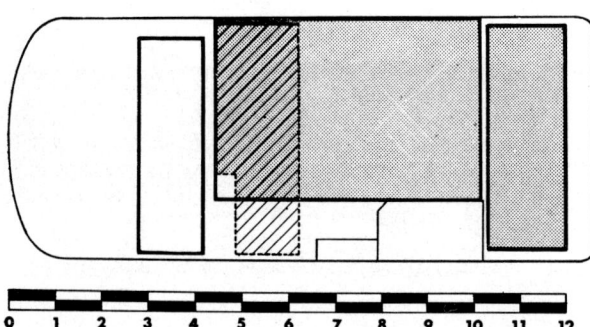

0 1 2 3 4 5 6 7 8 9 10 11 12

Sleeping   Two adults (in double bed) plus two children, one of whom sleeps in a bunk.

THE introduction last year of the bigger 1,500 c.c. engine for the Volkswagen Kombi, de Luxe and Standard Micro Bus brought a new dimension to motor-caravanning. Without sacrificing its well-known driving comfort, quietness and economy, the Volkswagen now offers performance which is in the GT class by motor-caravan standards.

The Devon Caravette offers less interior space than most other motor-caravans, but it is an ideal choice for the man who wants a nimble family car for most of the year, and a caravan for spring and summer weekends and holidays, without the expense of two vehicles.

As a comfortable, long-legged and economic family tourer, the 1,500 c.c. Devon Caravette has few equals.

The Volkswagen Micro Bus

The Devon Caravette we tested was based on a standard Micro Bus. This machine is unusual among the vans on which motor-caravans are based in having independent suspension all round, a rear engine and synchromesh on all four gears. The 1½-litre engine was virtually inaudible except when accelerating hard, though there was a little transmission whine at higher cruising speeds. The driving position was relaxed and comfortable, but the floor-mounted gear lever and handbrake are a long reach away from tall people. All the controls are light and positive, though the steering at low speeds and over bad surfaces feels vague and spongy till you get used to it.

In heavy traffic and around country lanes the Micro Bus is as nimble as most family saloons, but it is on the open road that one discovers the value of the bigger engine. This motor-caravan really comes to life at speeds where most others are running out of breath or roadholding. Cruising speeds in the 70s can be held for mile after mile when traffic conditions allow. And this with none of the engine noise one usually associates with forward-control vans at speed. The choice of gear ratios plays a large part in keeping down engine speeds, with third gear a useful "town top" and fourth almost an overdrive.

This standard of performance emphasized one of the main criticisms of almost all caravan conversions—barely adequate braking. Though the brakes of the Volkswagen are as good as those of any van we have tested recently, those at the rear locked all too readily in emergency stops from high speeds. This van is also

Interior of the Devon Caravette is well finished and rugged. No rattles developed on the road, and seats, tables and beds were all easy to erect and dismantle.

very sensitive to gusty crosswinds when cruising at more than 60 m.p.h.

The overall fuel consumption of 26 m.p.g. reflects maximum use of the van's high cruising speed, plus a good deal of about-town driving. Most owners could expect to improve on this.

Ancillary equipment included electric wipers which left an awkward blind area in the centre of the two-piece windscreen, an excellent electric screenwasher (extra), and a none-too-powerful fresh air heater.

The Devon Caravette Conversion

The Volkswagen forward-control van is the most difficult machine of its type to convert into a motor-caravan, as the bulkhead behind the front seats and the bulge over the rear engine leaves comparatively little clear floor space. The Devon Caravette finds a satisfactory compromise by assuming that under most conditions owners will cook and wash under the awning at the side of the van. Side curtains are in fact available as extras to turn the space under the awning into a draughtproof living area. Beds for two adults and two children are provided in the body of the van.

This type of conversion emphasizes the fact that the Volkswagen will appeal most to those who prefer a touring holiday. For an extra £136 a Martin Walter extending roof offers more headroom, two more full-size beds and a good deal more air space, but motor-caravanners who demand maximum in-the-van living space rather than performance and mobility must look elsewhere.

In practice the conversion is logical and well-executed. The beds are easy to make up and very comfortable, and meals in the van are no problem if the cooker (with grill and two burners) is moved to its optional position on the side door. For travelling there are four forward and two rear-facing passenger seats. Two tables are provided, the larger of which is for meals outside the van.

Great pains have been taken over sound and heat insulation, though the parcel shelf under the facia is a bad condensation trap. The van we tested was also fitted with a useful spring-out step under the side doors, but the front doors did not hold open and no handles were provided to aid entry into the cab. There is not a great deal of storage space, but there is a wardrobe, a heated blanket compartment under the rear seat and a small cooler sufficient for day-to-day supplies of milk, butter, etc. All-round curtains are standard.

Cooker surround folds flat for travelling. Plastic basin is used for washing, fed by a fold-away pump-type tap.

Left hand side door carries well-fitted, rattle-free lockers for crockery and cutlery.

IN BRIEF

Price	£1,080	
Manufacturer	J. P. White (Sidmouth) Ltd. U.K. Concessionaires: Lisburne Garage, Alexandria Works, Sidmouth, Devon.	
Capacity	Sleeping—4; Touring—7	
Dimensions (Overall)	Length	14 ft. 0½ in.
	Width	5 ft. 9 in.
	Height	6 ft. 4 in.
Engine	4 cylinder; 1,493 c.c.; 51 b.h.p. at 4,000 r.p.m.	
Fuel consumption	At steady	
	30 m.p.h.	46.5 m.p.g.
	40 m.p.h.	37.7 m.p.g.
	50 m.p.h.	32.2 m.p.g.
	Overall	26 m.p.g.
Acceleration	0-30 m.p.h.	8.2 sec.
	0-40 m.p.h.	15.5 sec.
	0-50 m.p.h.	22.5 sec.
Braking	Pedal pressure	Stopping distance from 30 m.p.h.
	25 lb.	131 ft.
	50 lb.	73 ft.
	75 lb.	48 ft.
	95 lb.	43 ft.
At higher pressures the rear wheels lock.		

THE COMPLEAT CAMPER

YOURS THROUGH THIS DETAILED PHOTO STORY

ALEX WALORDY

▶ When the first rays of Spring sunshine filter through the window, even the hardest working executives begin to cast longing glances to the outside, and you can certainly count on their wives and children to do the same. Touring in style and staying at the finest motels can become a bit of a drag, so why not a camper? You can buy them right off the show room floor with everything, including the kitchen sink. They only cost ... Well gee, for that price we could stay at the finest motels for the next three summers and have money left over. Let's build it.

Now in most instances this spells: "Famous Last Words". By the time you add up the hours out into even a fairly modest project, and multiply this by the going coolie wage, you are already past the new item, cost, not counting materials. As experienced do-it-yourselfers, we can vouch for this one. About this time the hobbyist performs a bit of mathematical legerdemain, and writes off the time as "recreation", a practice that sets accounting methods back 200 years. You might rationalize your way out of it if you work for a fixed stipend during regular hours and your boss hasn't heard of overtime. However, even this excuse

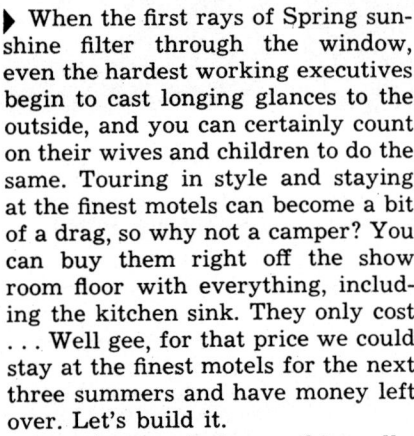

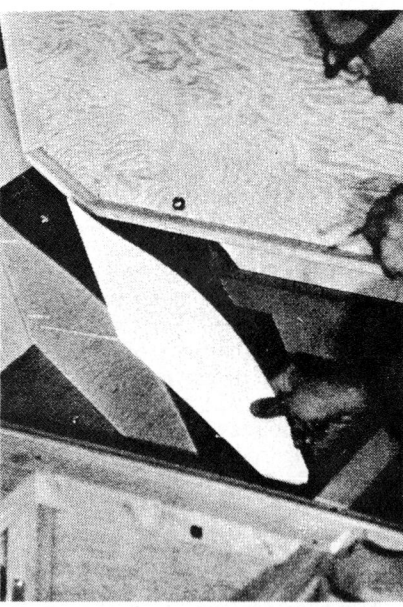

Prefinished plywood paneling is available at a very moderate cost from lumber yards. You can save money by purchasing panels with small edge damage, unsuitable for major home decoration, but perfect for the quilt work of small pieces needed inside a wagon. The underside of all bunk and seat areas also doubles as storage space. Curved section around the wheel housings is covered with masonite. All panels are retained with parker screws and chrome washers.

Wherever possible make cardboard templates first, then transfer the outline to plywood, masonite or whatever material you want to cut. This is easier than trying to fit a piece directly. In this instance, one template served for both wheel housings. Most of a project of this type can be completed with a plain hand saw and a miter box. Work will proceed much faster if you invest in a powersaw, available from any hardware store, or from Sears, for a modest cost.

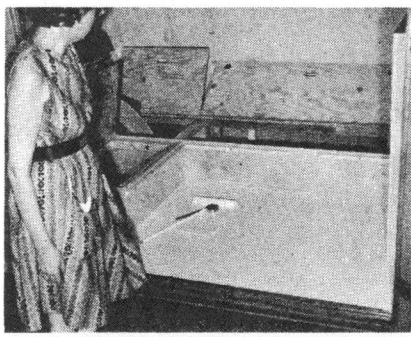

Insulation is an important step in the building of a camper. Volks heat being designed for the more temperate climes, a few fiberglass battens can't hurt. In fact on this job insulation was installed under every panel. Plastic cement painted on the batten covering, and on the panel provides a ready made method of adhesion till the panel is installed.

The floor was covered with masonite and finished with plastic tiles. They are easy to keep clean, brighten the interior and make it fairly track proof at camping time. Piano hinges are used at all of the storage trap doors and elongated holes offer a convenient handgrip. Handles would have interfered with the cushions.

A bunk is, of course, the most important part of a camper. The upper bunk was designed so that it would fold down against the side, forming a back rest for a sofa during the day. This called for a folding support such as this hinge leg. You can buy it at a lumber yard or borrow it from an old card table.

You don't have to coat the entire batten with stickum. Just paint a few stripes that will help hold it. Readily available corner moldings are used to trim the plywood edges. In your plans, make allowances for a set of additional windows with built in wire screens. They are an absolute must if you are converting a transporter.

Before you complete the roof, do provide some electrical outlets, as well as strips that will help fasten the roof paneling. The lip running along the inside roof rail provides a good place for anchoring the insulation and the headlining that will cover it. The insulation will have to be supported till the cement takes. Patience please.

There are times when you do need four hands for a job like this. Headliner panels can be paired to each other by providing a bonding strip inside the roof and screwing both panels to it. The joint is covered with chrome or aluminum trim. You can also short cut, using only the aluminum trim and retain it to the panels with wood or parker oval head screws, as was done here.

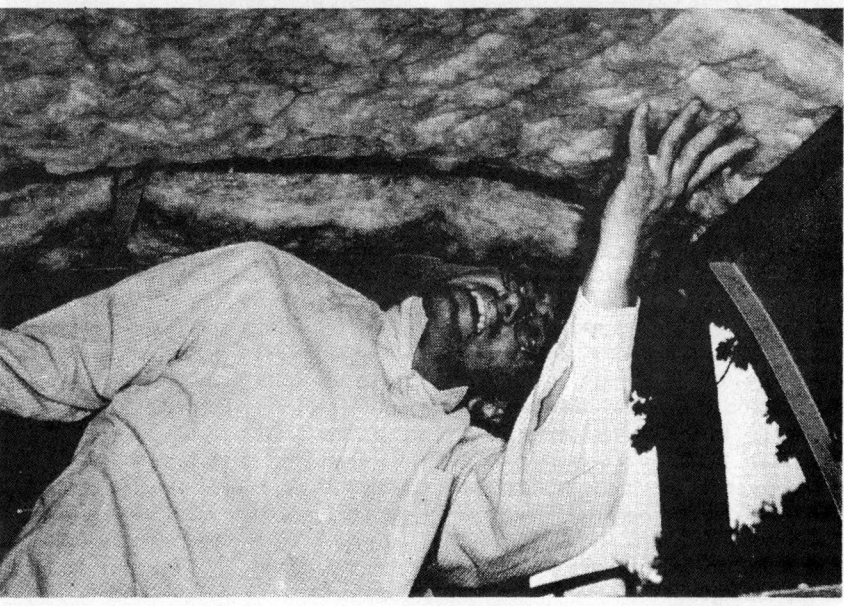

COMPLEAT CAMPER

The plywood base of the bunk is trimmed with boards that will retain the mattress in position. The front of the bunk will rest on the top of the cabinet, while the folding leg will support the rear. A length of tubing fastened to the rear of the bunk engages a set of hinge straps and prevents the bunk from sliding out.

Blocks of polyurethane foam were bought at a specialty store, precut to size. Additional trimming can be done with a sharp knife or a saw, but it is hard to cut it accurately without the professional equipment. Material is pinned up, and the seams marked out. Always make reference marks so corresponding pieces can be aligned. Make the cover tight, so the foam will fill it out completely. A few dabs of water here and there can work out wrinkles in the finished product.

doesn't seem to apply to Gus Pawelka, a designer of toys and motion displays, who can hardly find enough days in the week as it is.

There is only one way out of a dilemma like this: plan carefully and eliminate all frills that are not absolutely necessary. Screws are used in many joints that would normally be dovetailed and glued. Edge moldings and special miters have been kept at a minimum. On the other hand, the workmanship is clean and the maximum storage space has been built in. The wagon is fully insulated and trimmed with prefinished plywood paneling. The building of the camper eventually turned into a family project, with Ruth Pawelka, a talented jewelry designer taking over the complete interior trim, from fabric selection on to the last stitch. The project was subdivided into several stages with the total working time being under two weeks. The results were recorded by camera eye and there has been no living in my house since then because of several vocal forces in favor of a similar project. ●

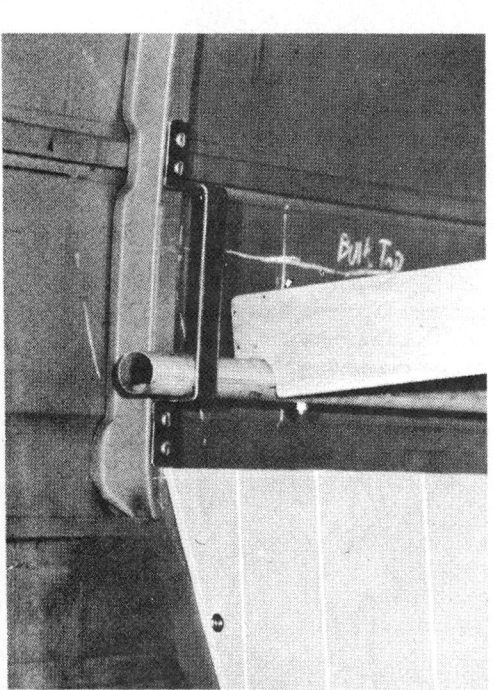

The bunk was made fairly wide, for comfort. Yet, there were some definite limitations on how high it could be hinged and still allow adequate head clearance. The solution was very simple; a pair of these straps, bent in a vise and secured to the wall with sheet metal screws, allows the bunk to slide up and fold when used as a back rest. Aluminum caps were used to cover the ends of the tubing.

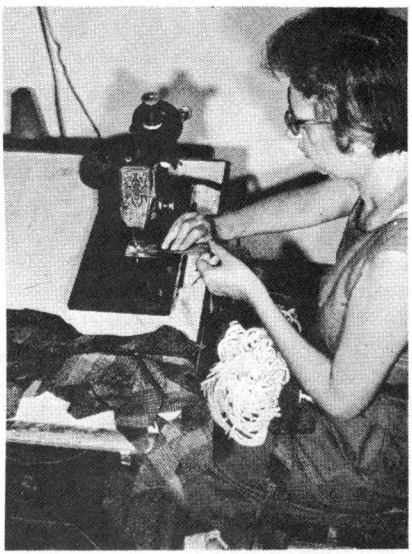

No need for a large professional machine to do the job. Cord and scrap strips of the parent material are used to make up welting. A special attachment on the machine helps keep a straight line when sawing welting or completing a seam. The pieces of material are placed face to face, with the thick portion of the welting in between. When the section is unfolded, the thick portion of the welting hides the seam and protects it.

Gee, Dad, this is pretty comfortable . . . Small notch had to be taken out of the lower cushion to clear the wheel housing. Front cushion can be used as a back rest and the wooden support folded out of the way, increasing the floor space. You'll see more of the same support, because it is also a very versatile table.

The upper bunk has been folded down, and the table is half extended, forming a cozy study or breakfast nook. Pattern on the fabric was successfully picked and gives the impression of a much larger interior. One by one square stock attached to the base board serves as a retainer for the table when it is used as a bunk.

Some pretty exotic cargo can be carried over a flat four engine . . . Bars help retain luggage or can be used as clothes hangers. ➔

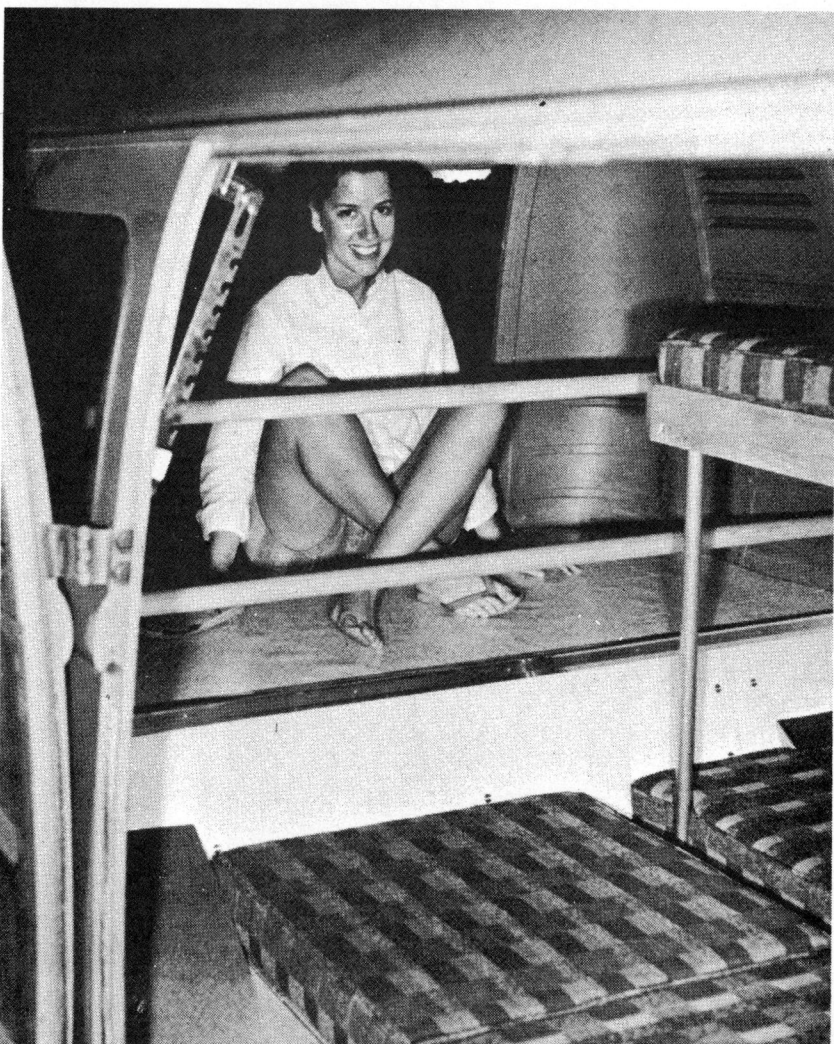

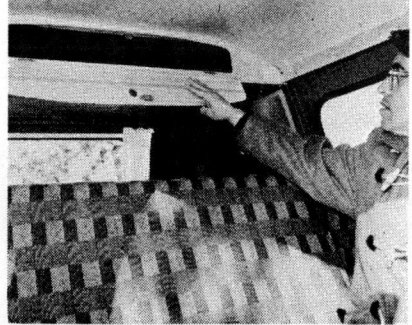

The end of the headliner would involve difficult compound curves. It was just as easy to finish off with a flat panel and add a practical storage space to boot.

Set of curtains were the inevitable homey touch added by the ladies of the house. Price of a Volks gas gauge was spent on reserve can instead. ➔

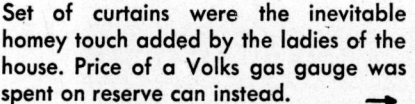

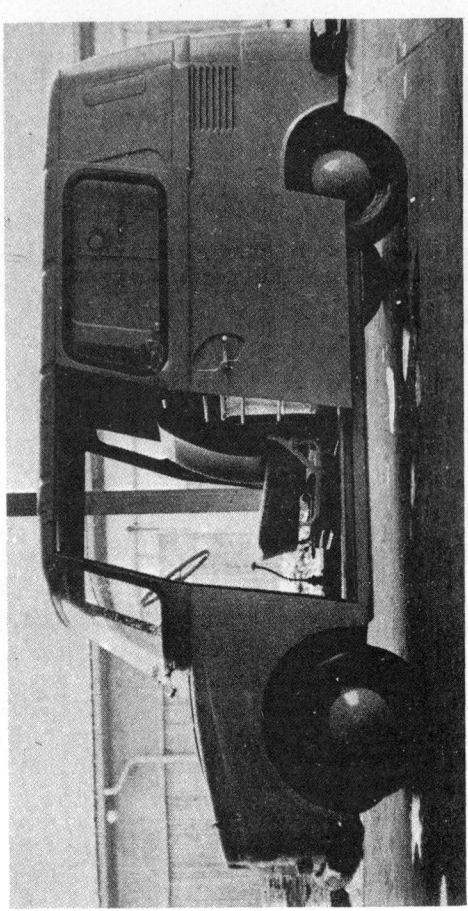

Rear door is somewhat reminiscent of the larger VW Kombi. but instead of torsion bar springs it has a prop bar.

Doors slide back along the outside of the vehicle making it easy to get a wide opening in a narrow street. Unlike some sliding doors I have known, these glide back smoothly at a touch. This is real walk-through convenience.

NEW VW VAN

By SLONIGER

Here's a brand new box-type Beetle.

▲ "A new body style from Wolfsburg?" Right. "On the VW 1200 frame?" Right again. "And nobody is blowing trumpets or scattering rose petals?" Correct for the third time. "Never," You are wise beyond your years, sad to tell. There *is* a new variation on the beetle, and it *is* acknowledged by Wolfsburg but the Westfalia Kleinlieferwagen (or mini-van) is not *the* new VW.

To set the record straight Westfalia, the people who make VW Campers among other things, are just beginning to turn out regular supplies of a city delivery van with VW 1200 power to more or less fill a niche between the sedan and the Kombi. If that was the whole tale we could close the report here but the van takes on added lustre because papa Wolfsburg has taken it under

The first two or the new VW 1200 Kleinlieferwagens or mini-vans drive out of the Westfalia factory gates headed for service with the German Post Office.

62

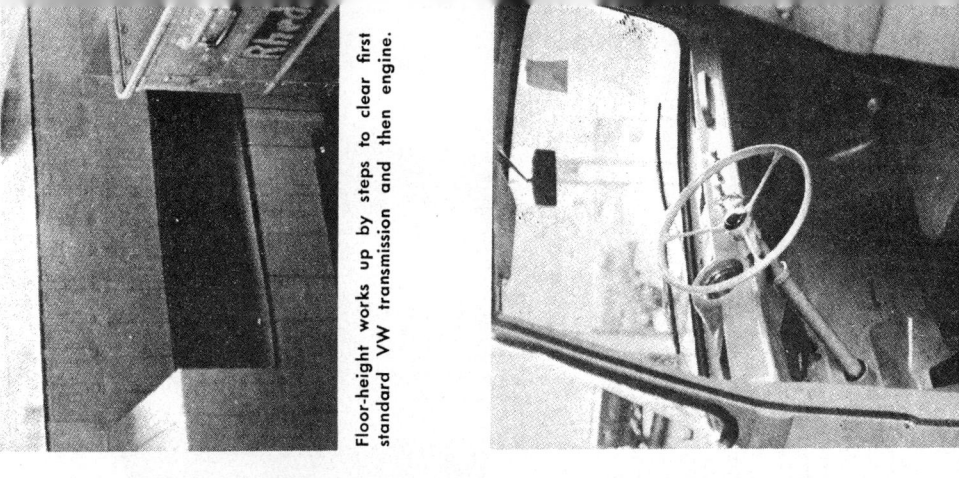

Floor-height works up by steps to clear first standard VW transmission and then engine.

VW Van returns to an old favorite, the flip-lever reserve system instead of a gas gauge.

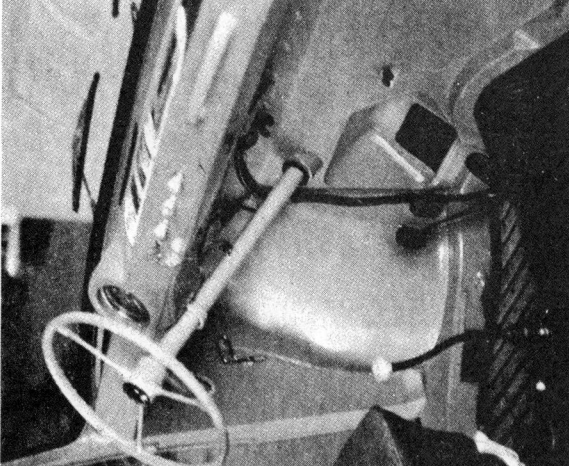

Stark office has duck-board floor and no frills with key for rear door like Kombi's.

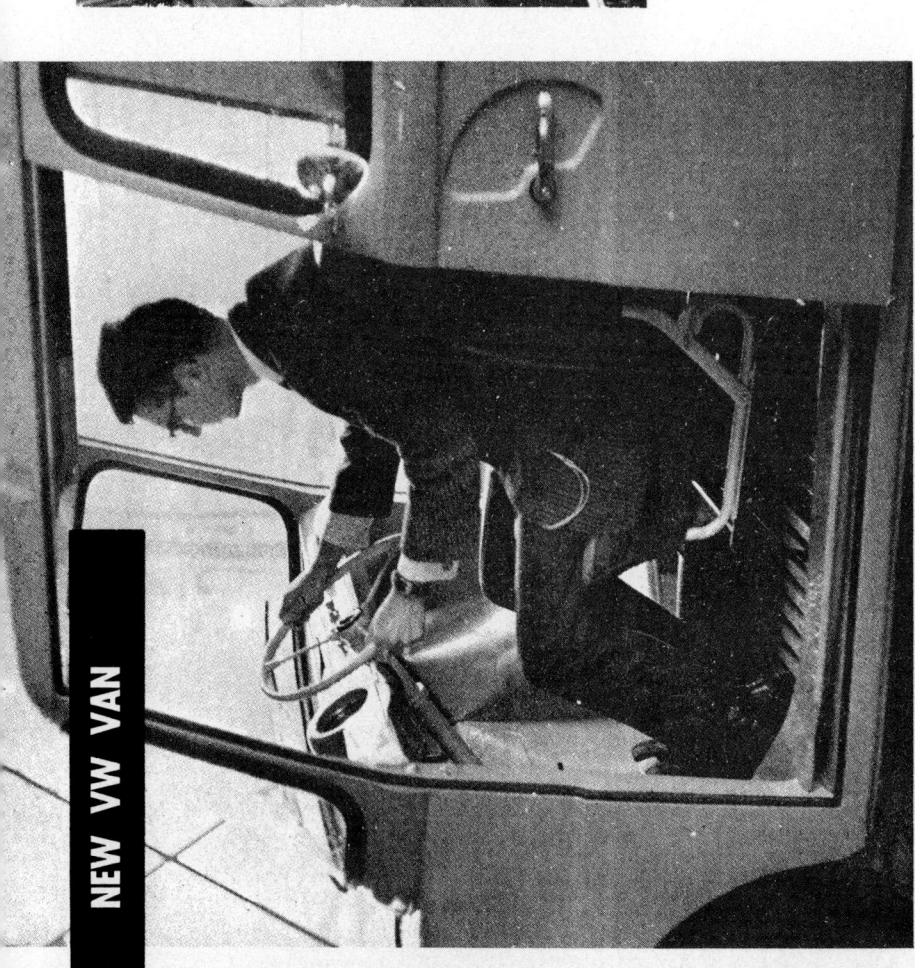

Upright seat has adjustable back rest and intermediate wheel angle for business-like driving.

the family wing. Not only do they recognize the van's existence, meaning it will be serviced at VW dealers, but they are handling the sales as well.

More explicitly, they will be handling the sales when Westfalia can produce enough of them to serve private desires. The first vehicles off their small production line are designed for the German Post Office—hence the insignia in our pictures—but there is every intent to satisfy the small wave of private inquiries too. As a matter of fact the local PO

isn't even allowed to buy a special vehicle—only those commercially available to other customers—so we are assured of regular deliveries soon.

Apparently even VW and Westfalia were slightly surprised at the number of people who want a van of these dimensions. Already there is talk of taking workers off trailer production to expand van production —while VW has turned a certain number of their famous inspectors loose to live in Wiedenbrueck and watch over the van output.

To anybody who knows the quality

standards of the Westfalia VW Campers this is typical double checking. Those have always been fully up to parent VW levels and the four vans I examined are equally well screwed together. The high standards are apparent in things like the sliding side doors which actually slide at a touch and seat in the closed position with that quality thunk.

In short, Westfalia has been known for some 120 years as a producer of quality goods, from coaches in the beginning to the trailer line founded over three decades back. Since 1951 they have also produced VW Campers, now at a rate of ten daily. Wolfsburg had every reason to pay special attention to the Westfalia van idea.

There is considerable coyness when you ask who actually designed the new mini-van but there is no closed season on educated guesses. I would think Westfalia had the original plan but they hasten to add the final form was decided in concert with VW,

NEW VW VAN

engine. On the other hand there are many small businesses in need of door-to-door delivery service for small packages or maybe marmosets. They don't need the size and unwieldyness of the Kombi but would love the VW reliability. Curb-height driver doors will be appreciated by their pilots too.

Even a quick look at the van layout and compactness, while thinking of such metropolitan needs (and traffic jams) and you wonder only that nobody got such a good idea before. Even VW is now moving to fill more gaps in their line. Since the Kombi went to 1.5 liters the need for a smaller delivery vehicle must have been obvious—except it took Westfalia to think of it.

By reducing overall bulk they achieve roughly the same performance in the van with a 1.2 liter engine as the larger Kombi with 1.5 liters. Both are rated at some 60 mph depending on the way the wind is blowing. On the plus side for the van it produces its 60 on only a fraction
CONTINUED ON PAGE 95

while the PO had a considerable hand in detail planning. Actually Westfalia is keyed to produce batches of vans with almost any interior fittings but we'll stick to the basic unit here.

Using a Karmann Ghia chassis—another point they didn't seem to have a reason for—they fit the standard 34 DIN hp VW 1200 engine and all-synchro gearbox. These are wrapped in a boxy body with a vestigal nose which is a styling conglomeration of the Kombi in back, the 1200 in the front fenders and a shorter 1500 in the nose panel. Sliding doors are a special option on one sort of Kombi, the rear lid which lifts and locks in two upper positions parallels that of the bigger van as well.

If your moving chores include large refrigerators or Shetland ponies for instance, the Kombi is still your best VW bet, particularly now that they use the 1.5 liter version of the old

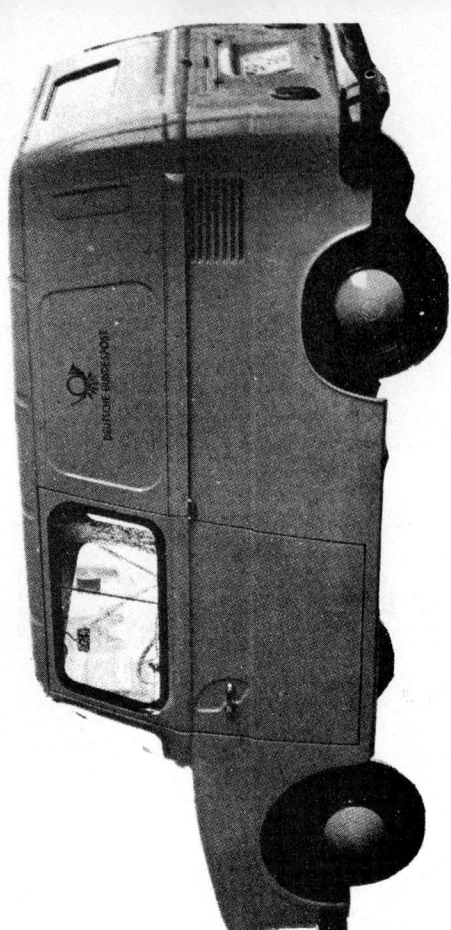

Fresh washed and dripping wet, VW Van is now ready for the Deutsches Bundespost.

Package bin behind diver's seat is a P.O. extra, one of many interior options that will be available on later "civilian" versions. These will be produced when the P.O. contract is complete.

Tank, spare, tool roll, and jack nearly fill up nose luggage space, but then this vehicle is not a family conveyance which might need a traveling closet built into one end or the other.

MOST *improved VW—*
BUS

DEAN OSTER'S $12,000 VW BUS/CAMPER SPORTS IDEAS YOU CAN USE TO IMPROVE ANY VW BUS — BE IT PLAIN OR FANCY

By THE EDITOR

▶ The contest for the Most Improved VW Bus is sometimes even more interesting than that for the Most Improved Sedan. At this year's VW Club of America Convention in St. Louis this was the case, but not because the sedans were uninteresting. It was just that the winner and runner up had been seen in other contests. But most of the buses entered in this year's contest had not been at the New York convention while many of last year's top buses stayed in the far off if not mysterious East.

The winning bus was the most expensive on display, but it was not money ($10,000-12,000) invested in his winner that earned Dean Oster his cup—it was the thought and design that he employed.

Outwardly this looked like a normal VW Station Wagon converted into a camper or perhaps equipped with one of the fancier camper kits now on the market. However, looks can be deceiving. The empty shell of the bus was built to Dean's specifications after a two-year struggle to get VW to build the bus he wanted. Non-stock items include such things as the fire engine (yes, the VW truck can be had as

From the front, Dean Oster's special bus looks pretty stock, but door art makes it stand out.

![Dog Patch Express VW Bus side view](top image)

MOST IMPROVED VW BUS

Ready for the road, "Dog Patch Express" has furled awning, full water and propane tanks in box on roof-rack and three antennae for radio (center nose), CB radio (left nose), and TV (roof).

The line of the air conditioner matches bus roof line tumblehome so you have to look twice to see raised area.

Three-quarter rear view shows fuel and water tank on roof-rack reached by ladder. Hump under rack is air conditioner, round tank holds air supply for horns mounted on rack, and vents behind driver's door are for gas operated refrigerator.

RIGHT: Inside driver's compartment, you begin to see extent of modifications. Belts and harness aim for safety while CB radio and soft drink tray between seats with under-dash rack add interest and convenience for trips.

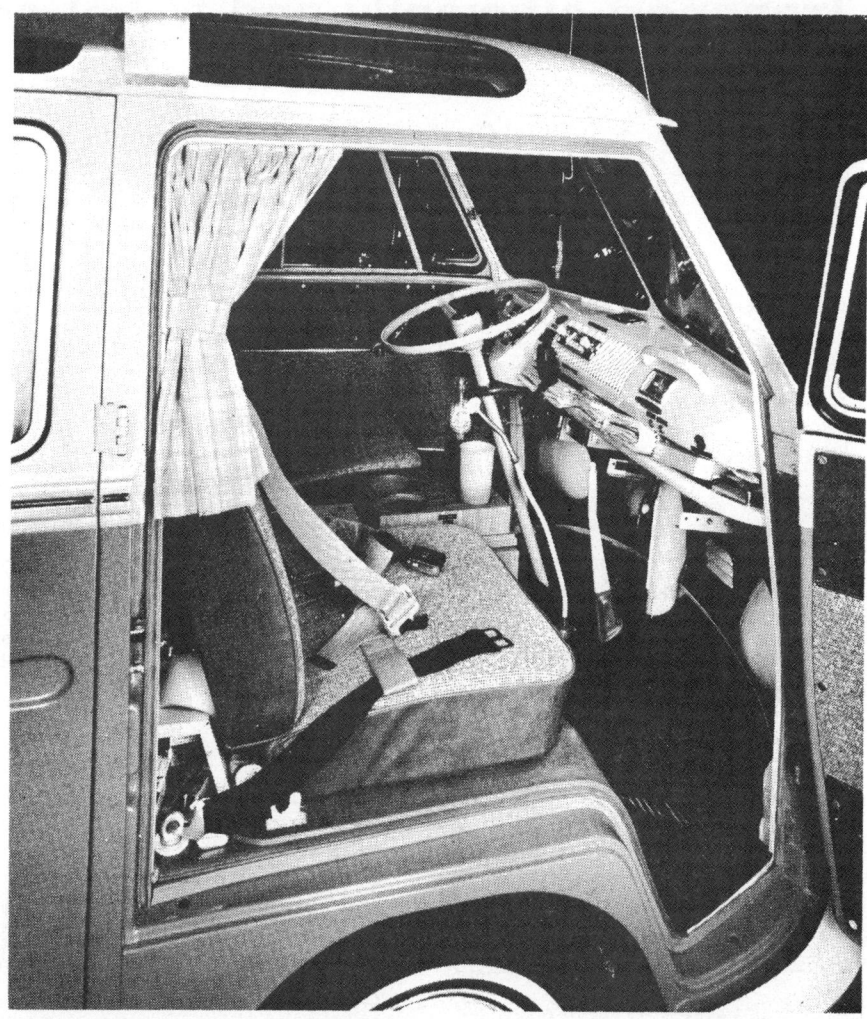

a fully equipped fire engine) under body supports and extra framing plus the ambulance springing and shock absorbers. In the right rear corner of the engine compartment he has a large extra battery to help handle the added electrical loads, but otherwise the basic machinery has been left strictly stock.

Where things get completely unstock is in the design of the camper inside the bare shell they received from Wolfsburg. Dean and his family designed and redesigned to make room in this standard-sized VW bus for sleeping accomodations for four, hot and cold running water, refrigeration, a shower, flush toilet with holding tank, two way radio, television, high fidelity, air conditioning—in short all the comforts of home and some that most homes do not yet boast. Yet all this equipment fits in and on the bus which is far handier and more maneuverable than a trailer or one of the larger Motor Homes as some are called.

On the roof, he has his fuel and water supply. This comes to almost 400 pounds of extra weight mounted high at the back. When I first saw this vehicle, I was frankly frightened by what I imagined its handling qualities might be. But when I got a chance to drive it for perhaps 10 miles, I found that this is indeed a usable machine. At very slow speeds on narrow back roads with a high crown, you can feel the weight. It sort of throws the bus from one side to the other as your cross the crown of the road and gave me the same unstable feeling as a bicycle I had as a boy. The basket was mounted on top of the rear fender which gave it much the same unbalanced feeling when loaded with papers. But once on the highway, this feeling departed and I was amazed by the general steadiness and well controlled road behavior. Taking a sweeping off-ramp to another expressway, the bus would settle into its turn and simply hold on without the least bit of skittishness.

RIGHT: Every switch and control is neatly labeled, a necessity for any driver not familiar with them.

I had also thought that the greatly increased weight might make this a slow menace on a high speed road. In this I was also wrong. As with all the Kombi family, it was no speed demon, but it would cruise easily at about 55 mph and on a grade it would hold 50 mph if you pushed the accelerator to the floor and held it there. Getting started was also a matter of flooring it and building up the revs in each gear so

you could hit the torque peak for the upshift. But then this vehicle has a truck in its ancestry, and it was designed to handle heavy loads. Perhaps it was not meant to handle loads quite this heavy, but it can and does it competently. A sports car it is not, but a useful vehicle it most certainly is.

Even more impressive than the fact that it drives and rides pretty well is the way it is organized so

CONTINUED ON PAGE 81

Transport efficiently and travel comfortably. Why?

VW Delivery Van

	Unladen weight	1,070 kg [1]	(2,359 lb [1])
	Payload	1,000 kg	(2,205 lb)
	Permissible total weight	2,070 kg	(4,564 lb)

4.8 m³ = 170 ft³
1925 mm = 75.8 in   1170 mm = 46.1 in
200 mm = 7.9 in   4280 mm = 168.5 in   1750 mm = 68.9 in
1230 mm = 48.4 in   2700 mm = 106.3 in   1350 mm = 53.1 in   2700 mm = 106.3 in
730 mm = 28.7 in   485 mm = 19.1 in   1200 mm = 47.2 in   1500 mm = 59.1 in

☐ 4,8 m³

VW High Roofed Delivery Van

	Unladen weight	1,110 kg [1]	(2,447 lb [1])
	Payload	960 kg	(2,117 lb)
	Permissible total weight	2,070 kg	(4,564 lb)

6.0 m³ = 212 ft³
730 mm = 28.7 in   1680 mm = 66.1 in
970 mm = 38.2 in   1570 mm = 61.8 in
900 mm = 35.4 in   200 mm = 7.9 in   4280 mm = 168.5 in   1750 mm = 68.9 in
730 mm = 28.7 in   2700 mm = 106.3 in   1170 mm = 46.1 in   2700 mm = 106.3 in
485 mm = 19.1 in   2285 mm = 90.0 in   1500 mm = 59.1 in

☐ 6,0 m³

VW Pick-up without/with tarpaulin and bows

	Unladen weight	1,085/1,120 kg [1]	(2,392/2,469 lb [1])
	Payload	985/950 kg	(2,172/2,095 lb)
	Permissible total weight	2,070 kg	(4,564 lb)

4.2 m² = 45 ft²   970 mm = 38.2 in   1750 mm = 68.9 in
0.65 m³ = 23 ft³   200 mm = 7.9 in   1570 mm = 61.8 in
4.55 m³ = 161 ft³   340 mm = 13.4 in   1600 mm = 63.0 in
1200 mm = 47.2 in   4290 mm = 168.9 in   2600 mm = 102.4 in
375 mm = 14.8 in   1910 mm = 75.2 in   1200 mm = 47.2 in

☐ 4,2 m²   ▨ 0,65 m³   ☐ 4,55 m³

VW Pick-up with enlarged platform

	Unladen weight	1,130 kg [1]	(2,491 lb [1])
	Payload	940 kg	(2,073 lb)
	Permissible total weight	2,070 kg	(4,564 lb)

5.04 m² = 55 ft²   200 mm = 7.9 in   2020 mm = 79.5 in   1200 mm = 47.2 in
0.65 m³ = 23 ft³   340 mm = 13.4 in   1910 mm = 75.2 in
375 mm = 14.8 in   4290 mm = 168.9 in   1600 mm = 63.0 in
970 mm = 38.2 in   1910 mm = 75.2 in   2600 mm = 102.4 in

☐ 5,04 m²   ▨ 0,65 m³

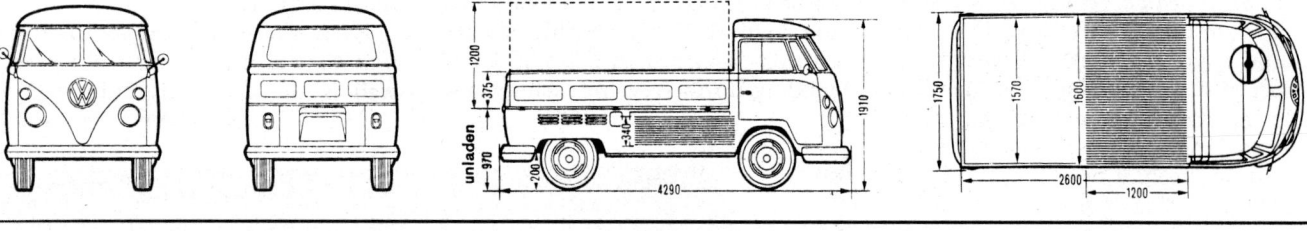

[1] including driver   [2] with 5 seats unoccupied   [3] including driver and seats

68

Because the VW range caters for every need.

VW Double Cab Pick-up without/with tarpaulin and bows

Unladen weight 1,130/1,150 kg [1] (2,491/2,535 lb [1])
Payload   940/920 kg [2] (2,073 / 2,029 lb [2])
Permissible
total weight   2,070 kg   (4,564 lb)

2.75 m² = 30 ft²	970 mm = 38.2 in	1750 mm = 68.9 in
4.9 m³ = 173 ft³	200 mm = 7.9 in	1570 mm = 61.8 in
1200 mm = 47.2 in	4290 mm = 168.9 in	1755 mm = 69.1 in
375 mm = 14.8 in	1910 mm = 75.2 in	

2,75 m²   4,90 m³

 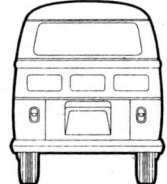 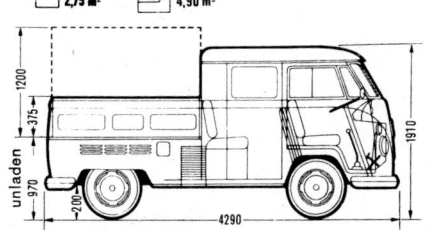 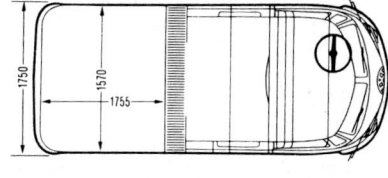

VW Kombi, VW Micro Bus

Unladen weight   1,140 kg [3/4] (2,514 lb [3/4])
Payload   930 kg   (2,050 lb)
Permissible
total weight   2,070 kg   (4,564 lb)

0.8 m³ = 28 ft³	485 mm = 19.1 in	1750 mm = 68.9 in
4.0 m³ = 142 ft³	4280 mm = 168.5 in	2700 mm = 106.3 in
1925 mm = 75.8 in	1350 mm = 53.1 in	1500 mm = 59.1 in
200 mm = 7.9 in		

1230 mm = 48.4 in
730 mm = 28.7 in

0,8 m³   4,0 m³

  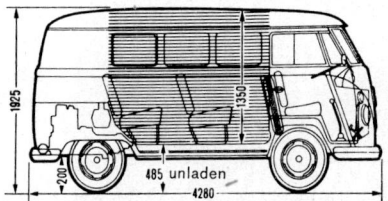 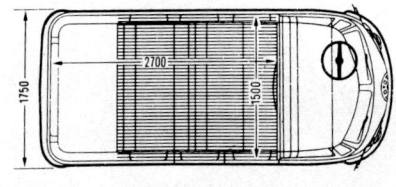

VW Micro Bus De Luxe

Unladen weight   1,150 kg [5] (2,535 lb [5])
Payload   920 kg   (2,029 lb)
Permissible
total weight   2,070 kg   (4,564 lb)

0.8 m³ = 28 ft³	200 mm = 7.9 in	1800 mm = 70.9 in
4.0 m³ = 142 ft³	485 mm = 19.1 in	1450 mm = 57.1 in
1925 mm = 75.8 in	1170 mm = 46.1 in	
830 mm = 32.7 in	1200 mm = 47.2 in	
900 mm = 35.4 in	4300 mm = 169.5 in	

1230 mm = 48.4 in
730 mm = 28.7 in

0,8 m³   4,0 m³

 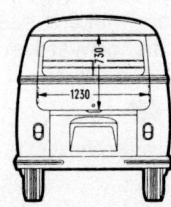 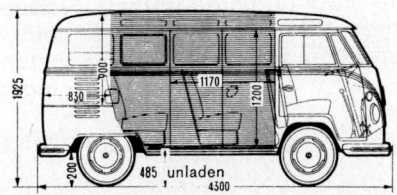 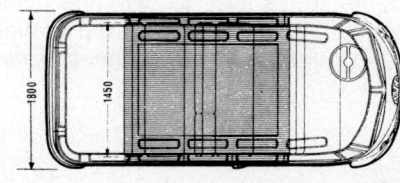

⁴ VW Micro Bus with seats and without driver — unladen weight 1,150 kg (2,535 lb), payload 920 kg (2,029 lb) ⁵ with seats and without driver

it's a caravan ◄

Getting away from it all for the weekend, or taking off with your family on a short holiday. Easy! When you escape in a VW Ten-Seater Kombi. A work-horse and business transporter during the week — a caravan for the weekend. There's loads of room for all your family, their equipment, tents, beds, chairs, fishing rods and the dog. Big accessible room inside with standing room for youngsters. Big storage room under the seats and behind the back seat. Comfortable driving cab. All round visibility over the top of the traffic.

it's a station wagon ◄

Surprise? The VW Ten-Seater Kombi takes the same number of people as two medium sized cars — but it's the price of only one (R1852 standard). But it's only nine inches longer than the VW beetle, so it's easy to park and manoeuvre. Easy on petrol too — around 30 m.p.g. A big, big station wagon that will take your family comfortably, economically, easily anywhere you want to go.

it's a business transporter

Ten's a crowd — but not in the VW Ten-seater Kombi. Three in front including the driver. Seven inside. The interior seats face one another across a wide aisle (nice for conversation) and the occasional side seat folds away flush when not in use. Wide double doors make it easy to step inside or out, and an upward-swinging rear door opens up on a 28 cu. ft. storage space for luggage. ▼

70

it's a beach cabin ▶

A lazy day in the sun brought to you and your friends by the courtesy of the VW Ten-Seater Kombi. The ideal beach cabin, changing room, carrying bag on wheels. You can eat in it, play in it, sleep in it, wander all over the countryside in it. When the fun's all over the cabin's easy to clean out. Washable Vinyl upholstery. Flat floor — just brush the sand out of the door.

it's the

VOLKSWAGEN TEN-SEATER KOMBI

One of the range of reliable, versatile Volkswagen transporters. Powered by a 1500 cc air-cooled, low-revving engine at the rear. Each wheel is independently sprung by torsion bars — road shocks are absorbed individually by each wheel and not passed on to the rest of the vehicle. Easy to drive with a gearbox from the VW 1600 Fastback, that is precise, light and

positive. Easy on tyres too, 25,000 to 30,000 miles on one set is not uncommon. Heater and fresh-air controls are standard equipment in all models of the VW Ten-Seater. Your local Volkswagen dealer will be happy to show you a range of accessories to make your Kombi more personal and more useful, roof racks, overriders and steps.

PURCHASE OR LEASE

The standard Ten-Seater Kombi costs R1852 and the de-luxe version R1913. Your local Volkswagen dealer will be happy to explain to you how you can lease a Ten-Seater without capital outlay.

FUNNY FROM

ABOVE: Lift the front end of a VW Bus clear of the ground? You're kidding. But with this Mini-Bus it's so light that you don't have to be Superman to pick it up.

Shrunken VWs? No just a VW station wagon that's been split and rejoined omitting the passenger area and floor. The other half is a super-long VW Bus.

▶ As a fellow who encounters a great variety of unusual Volkswagens, Bruce Deutsch ranks on a level with editors of Volkswagen enthusiast magazines. In his work in Riverside, California, at EMPI as the accessory firm's Public Relations Director (that's a euphemism for publicity man, says Deutsch), he comes in daily contact with Volkswagens that are beautiful, unique, bizarre, ugly, and odd ball.

"The funny car we love best," says Deutsch with a grin, "is the mini-wagon—even though the darn thing doesn't have any of our accessories on it." Owner of the mini-

VOLKS CALIF.

RIGHT: Wheelie VW Mini-Bus can be had any time on stock VW engine in low gear.

BELOW: Who's short now? Mini-Bus can park where even a standard Beetle won't find enough room. Mini's wheelbase has shrunk to a mere 46 inches

BOTTOM: Only the tail pipes give away this cute pickup with its Ford T fiber glass body. The works are, of course, stock VW.

wagon is the operator of a California wrecking yard who welded together the extreme front and rear ends of two Volkswagen deluxe station wagons. By using somewhat less than half of each wagon he produced an eye-catching novelty with a wheelbase of only 46 inches. By contrast, stock wheelbase is more than twice that dimension, or 94.5 inches.

Overall length of the Volks mini is about 120 inches. Highly maneuverable, the stubby modified wagon turns in a 20-foot circle, compared with 39 feet for its stock counterpart.

Shortening the wagon changed the weight-distribution, thereby producing a unique performance characteristic. The front of the mini is so light it can be lifted off the ground by a man of average strength, and a sudden burst of throttle produces a drag-strip wheel stand (front wheels lift off road) that is the greatest attention getting device

since the invention of the bikini bathing suit.

Deutsch knows of another interesting VW bus, which he describes as being "nothing much to look at because it's so much like a stock bus in outward appearance—but it's a supercharged tiger for performance." This bus derives its power from a modified Olds engine, rated at 250 hp in stock condition. The engine switch involved an Olds drive train, including hydro transmission. An Olds radiator was cleverly hidden so, on casual inspection, one detects no hint of the bus' hidden secrets.

The owner delights in accepting the challenges of unsuspecting teenagers in Buicks and Mustangs who want to race to the next stoplight. As the race starts and the kid hears the Olds engine's powerful roar and sees smoke rolling off the bus' rear tires he usually swallows his bubble gum and misses a shift in surprise.

Another of Deutsch's favorites is what appears to be a customized version of an old Ford Model T with pickup box all fancied up for a custom-car show. Actually, it's largely Volkswagen, including chassis and engine. The heavy stock VW sedan body was discarded in favor of a fiberglass T-bucket. Hood, fenders, and pickup box were fabricated of light-gauge metal. A canvas top completes the roadster-like modifications.

With weight reduced to 1500 pounds and the addition of special rear wheels mounting 9.50-by-15 tires this VW runs well in the loosely packed sand of California's desert and wilderness areas. Owner frequently trailers his sand buggy-roadster behind the air-conditioned family car until he reaches the wilderness areas that are impenetrable by motor vehicles other than buggies and four-wheel drive cars. ●

7 MONTHS IN A VW

Part One

By ERNST A. JAHN ■ My wife Edith and I decided to visit all Central and South American countries in our Volkswagen Camper as our share to the United Nations International Cooperation Year. We prepared for the trip for more than eight months, running into all sorts of problems with documentation and formalities. A $2,000 cash deposit had to be made to obtain the Carnet de Passage en Douanes, valuable for all South American countries, while Argentina required an additional $4,000 and Brazil $3,000 to enter their countries by automobile. This is a security bond guaranteeing that one will not sell the car in those countries. A VW Camper in Chile, for example, is worth $10,000. The sums were refunded upon our return.

We left cold New York in December and returned

7 months later, after passing through 5 seasons, 21 foreign countries and driving 27,888 miles plus 270 miles by ship from Panama to Columbia and 4,066 miles by plane for the last leg of the return trip from Belem, Brazil to New York. We had spent $507 for gasoline and wore out two sets of tires. Our troubles and adventures were plentiful as we followed the Pan American Highway through Central and around South America as far as we possibly could go: Belem on Brazil's mighty Amazon delta. We never slept in hotels and, with half-a-dozen exceptions, did not eat in restaurants. A 2½ gallon portable water tank and two spare wheels were our reserves. The tank we frequently replenished in ostensibly "safe" areas.

We had only the most necessary spare parts with

CAMPER

A YOUNG HUSBAND/WIFE TEAM TAKE THEIR VOLKSWAGEN CAMPER FROM NEW YORK VIA THE ENTIRE LENGTH OF THE PAN AMERICAN HIGHWAY TO BELEM IN BRAZIL WITH A MINIMUM OF EXPERIENCE.

LEFT: Edith and Ernst A. Jahn on Dona Marta with Sugar Loaf Mountain, Rio de Janeiro, Brazil in the background. ABOVE: Edith fixing a meal at night on foot of volcano Nevado de Toluca, Mexico in front of an open fire.

us for the car such as spark plugs and points, extra sealed-beam headlights, a few bulbs, an extra spare wheel assembly, a fan belt and a few miscellaneous items including electrical wire, a water hose (to replenish water tank), insulation tape and asbestos sheets (for emergency replacement of seals). We also brought an electric refrigerator of the 12V-110V Bernzomatic type. A 6V to 110V inverter produced the voltage necessary for the operation of the portable refrigerator on 110V. I could also use my electric shaver and tape recorder this way. The battery drainage was so low as to be negligible. What we should have taken along were extra inner tubes, a tire repair kit, extra heavy six ply tires, a set of shock absorbers and a spare generator.

The lowest point of travel was the Salton Sea area in California, 235 ft. below sea level, while our highest was the ski resort area of Chacaltaya just outside La Paz, Bolivia, 17,384 ft. 20 per cent of all our travel was above 10,000 ft. altitude in the Andean highlands. The Volkswagen motor was not adjusted for the high altitude roads of the Andes but the car climbed the steep grades of the world's highest highway from Lima to La Oroya with an astonishing ease. About 70 per cent of the roads were paved; the rest were gravel and cobblestones. During the trip we suffered a few times from colds in the icy high mountains, even though it was their summer season. While I was shaving one morning in Mexico I heard Edith's loud scream. I found her writhing on the ground near our camping place and immediately thought that she had been bitten

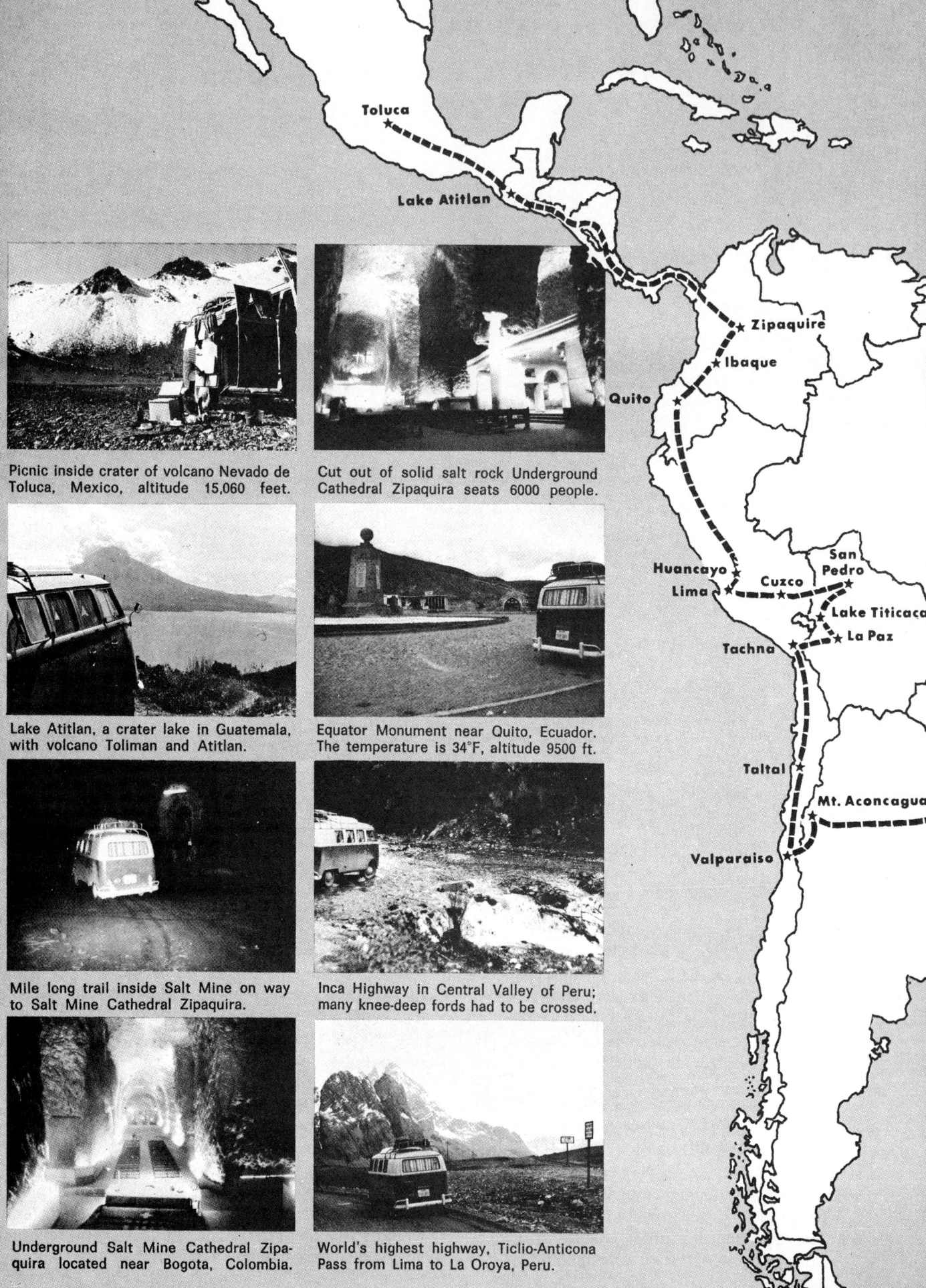

Picnic inside crater of volcano Nevado de Toluca, Mexico, altitude 15,060 feet.

Cut out of solid salt rock Underground Cathedral Zipaquira seats 6000 people.

Lake Atitlan, a crater lake in Guatemala, with volcano Toliman and Atitlan.

Equator Monument near Quito, Ecuador. The temperature is 34°F, altitude 9500 ft.

Mile long trail inside Salt Mine on way to Salt Mine Cathedral Zipaquira.

Inca Highway in Central Valley of Peru; many knee-deep fords had to be crossed.

Underground Salt Mine Cathedral Zipaquira located near Bogota, Colombia.

World's highest highway, Ticlio-Anticona Pass from Lima to La Oroya, Peru.

Toluca

Lake Atitlan

Quito

Zipaquire

Ibaque

Huancayo

Lima

Cuzco

San Pedro

Lake Titicaca

La Paz

Tachna

Taltal

Mt. Aconcagua

Valparaiso

7 MONTHS IN A VW CAMPER
Part One

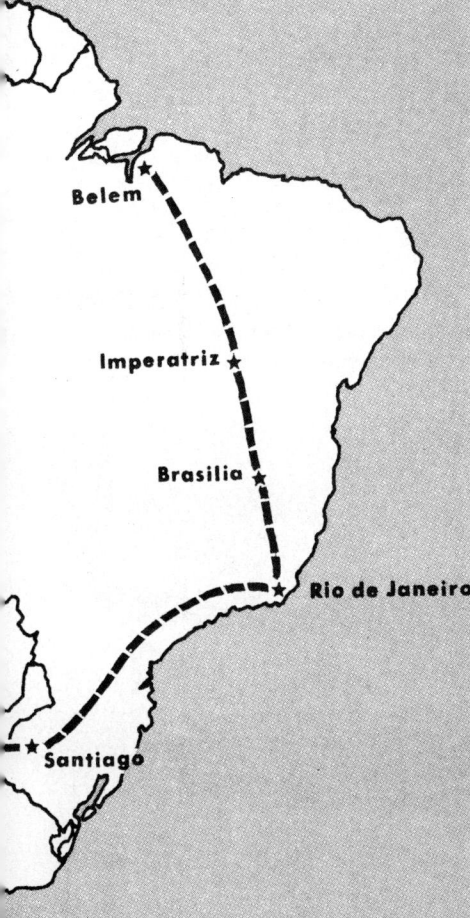

by a snake. "I tried to jump this ditch and slipped," she exclaimed half conscious. Relieved, I carried her to bed to treat a badly sprained ankle and served her an early morning cognac. Two days later my ex-ballet dancer wife, limping on one leg, managed to sprain the right ankle too, thus excluding herself from the driving schedule for the rest of Central America.

The highlight of our trip was the visit to the ruins of the ancient Inca Empire of Machu Picchu near the South American archaeological capital and sacred city of Cuzco, Peru. Here on the steep slopes of a mountain, embraced by the roaring Urubamba River, deeply hidden in tropical jungle, the Incas artfully carved and ingeniously fitted together massive stones without the aid of mortar. In Cuzco, poncho-clad indians lead their llama herds over narrow cobblestone streets and hold their open market in the city squares. A shiskebab of llama meat bought on one of those markets caused Edith to get a bad allergy. Days later in a desolate Lake Titicaca region her allergy accompanied by spells of high fever turned worse. No pharmacy . . . no doctor. . . . In a small village natives informed us of a first-aid station where an old Indian in a dark unclean room gave her a chlorine shot that fortunately helped. She was too sick to have objected.

People everywhere were quite surprised to see a foreign car equipped with bed, kitchen and refrigerator, not to mention the running water. Many times we were surrounded during lunch stops or in the evenings and had to demonstrate our mobile home. In the equator village of San Antonio a proud father of 20 children asked us whether we were married. When he learned that we have recently had our second anniversary and no children yet, he cheerfully comforted Edith: "Don't give up hopes." At one time we parked opposite a college in Ibague, Columbia, and while I was taking pictures nearby, 60-70 students swarmed around the VW, some offering their autographed pictures to Edith. I had a

hard time getting back to the car and even then they completely ignored me as her husband. This incident occurred in the midst of the dangerous Tolima Province where notorious bandits still kill people in villages and on highways in an undeclared civil war. Just a week before our arrival in this area bandits had held a raid and killed several natives in a large town. Even though we did not carry firearms we chanced this route, the only one we could travel south. Our nights were spent in the camper but always parked at gas stations between many long-distance trucks. Religious shrines alongside the highway indicated the execution of natives by rebels or location of fatal accidents on those ever twisting-winding-dropping and climbing roads.

We saw of course very little passenger car traffic, just trucks and busses overloaded with people and animals packed like sardines in a can. Had we taken along the many fare-offering hitchhikers we encountered, we could have recouped our travel expenses but experience told us never to pick up strangers. Some of the toll roads in Columbia were in such poor condition that we almost insisted on being paid for using them.

La Paz, Bolivia, the highest capital of the world is a gleaming gray city of faded red rooftops guarded by the towering snowy crest of Mount Illimani. We were thrilled by the spectacle of this picturesque town with its steep streets and breath-taking vistas. This city is noted for its lack of a fire department; even we had difficulties keeping a match or stove burning in this thin, cold air. Cut off from any ocean the country has all types of climates and 60 miles from La Paz we were swimming in rivers of the moist tropical Amazon basin. Most of the country's population consists of two types of Indians, the Quechuas and Aymaras. A visit to the pre-Inca Tiahuanaco monoliths and ruins gave us evidence of the life of two civilizations that once flourished here.

Inca Highway landslide near Urcos. Except for 2 shovels, no tools were used to clear road. Indians used hands.

Car and driver gets ride on rowboat-ferry across Lake Titicaca, Straits of Tiquina, a 3 km stretch.

EARTHQUAKES, FIRE IN THE ENGINE COMPARTMENT BESET OUR VW TRAVELLERS BUT STILL THEY PRESS ON!

7 MONTHS IN A VW CAMPER

Part Two

■ Between Lake Titicaca and the Peruvian coast, on a 200 mile gravel and sand road with altitudes ranging from 15,700 feet to 1,500 feet, we had one flat tire too many with no service station anywhere. Rather than having one of us stay behind with the car, we made the next 30 miles on three tires and the one rim we had as a second spare. We moved 40 mph on this drift-sand section to Tacna. The severely bent rim is presently being used by a Belem fisherman as a small boat anchoring weight.

Edith Jahn shows displaced papers after Chilean earthquake.

Edith prepares an evening meal on beach near Taltal, Chile.

Chile's border railway station Caracoles. Altitude: 10,500 ft.

Argentina's entrance gate at Las Cuevas on Pan Am Highway.

Passing through many hundred miles of the world's wildest arid region, the Atacama desert in northern Chile, with no rainfall ever to give life to anything, we reached Santiago where we witnessed the greatest tragedy of the trip, the March 28 earthquake. We sat in our car, parked on the beach near Valparaiso, 15 feet from the thundering South Pacific, when the 85 seconds tremor shook our car and displaced everything inside. We were panic-stricken when we realized what had happened and thought of the enormous tidal wave that followed the 1960 earthquake in southern Chile, flooding thousands of acres of land and causing great loss of life. We quickly tried to back up to higher land but of course the sand was soft and the wheels spun in. Panicky but helpful beachgoers noticed our calamity and helped to pull us out. Fortunately there was no tidal wave. The loss of homes and lives in the villages was extensive and the small mining town of El Cobre with 450 inhabitants was completely flooded by thousands of tons of copper-mud sludge after the tremor broke a dam; a shocking sight.

In Santiago we were in the midst of a student uprising in demonstration against a hike in bus fares, where police teargas made our eyes water, noses burn and throats tickle. We got out of Santiago in a hurry. Due to the earthquake, the weather pattern in Chile changed and brought an early rainy season and snow season up in the Andes which spoiled our visit to the Chilean Lake district. We crossed to Argentina through

the international railway tunnel instead of going over the pass which due to heavy snowfall was closed. Magnificent and impressive 22,834 ft. high Mount Aconcagua, the world's second highest mountain, towered over us while we passed within 10 miles of her leaving the mountains for the monotonous, flat Pampa.

Through Argentina and Uruguay we finally made Brazil, the land we never thought we would reach. It was a glorious feeling to enter Rio de Janeiro, the "Cidade Maravilhosa," as the Brazilians proudly call it. The Brazilian Touring Club gave us an official welcome to Rio's 400th anniversary celebration and congratulated us as the first U.S. registered car in a decade to arrive here officially, entirely via road.

The city of contrast offered us enough excitement, from tropical jungle mountains to the most beautiful beaches in the world such as Copacabana and Ipanema. The heavy traffic here is comparable with New York's. Parking violators, however, are treated with greater dispatch. The policemen deflate the tires and take away the valves. Most drivers are equipped with hand-pumps and spare valves to beat the inconvenience. A wrong left turn netted us a U.S. ten cent fine. On our way to northern Brazil, in the state of Mato Grosso we passed 8 feet high termite hills covering the fields by the thousands. These termites are known to tear down everything in their path when they start moving across the land. Modern Brasilia

Edith Jahn on Copacabana beach in Rio de Janeiro, standing on famous Avenida Atlantica.

was a disappointment—an empty city suffering from acute deterioration. Nobody wants to live here, it is too far away from the well-developed playgrounds of the coastal region. We do agree with most Brazilians that the basic idea of building a city in this area is wonderful, but not when the country is stricken by so much inflation and political turmoil.

Some 800 miles short of our final destination a fire in the engine compartment almost put an abrupt end to our trip. On the way to Belem in a thick jungle area of the Amazon basin, far from any population and help, a rag caught fire. This rag was to stop the heavy powder dust from entering the air filter which was short of oil and it accidentally touched the hot manifold. Quick action by throwing road sand on the

engine extinguished the flames before they could reach the gas tank. Most of the hoses and electrical cables were burned. We had no spare parts for such unforseen accidents. My ingenious wife came to the rescue with her idea of making hoses out of asbestos sheets stapled together. To replace the oil breather line we cut up our water hose. First-aid tape closed the gap on the carburetor intake hose. The electrical wires we replaced with wires we had with us. We worked four hours in 110° F. temperature. After a complete clean-out of the engine compartment—we had to spoon out the sand—we continued our travels. It was only after our return to New York that we replaced those temporary parts

with original ones! This was not the end of our misfortune, however. Two days later on this very same road the generator failed. The coils were burned and there was not a single technician in the area who could help us out. An Irish missionary we then happened to meet, helped us to buy an extra 6 volt battery at the only gasoline station around. The only one they had cost us a mere US $53. Fortunately the dry-charged battery was defective and the money was cheerfully (!) refunded. We made the 400 miles to Imperatriz the first city where we could find service, on the battery alone.

The only way to wash our laundry and have our daily bath was to follow the natives' custom, so we joined them in

the many rivers we passed. In hot northern Brazil we could not resist the cool waters although they are infested with carnivorous piranha fish, electric eel, crocodiles, snakes, oxfish and devil fish (sting-ray). Not even at night could they keep us weary travelers out of it. In this same area malaria and filariasis (elephantiasis) mosquitos were a plague. We did take malaria pills for prevention. Regular meals were cooked by Edith on our gasoline and alcohol stoves. Except for a few cans we had brought along, most vegetables and meats were inexpensively bought at native markets. From local people she learned to prepare many delicious specialties.

The last leg of our return trip started

in Belem, from which point we shipped the car back to New York. Then we took a jet to fly to Surinam, Guyana and Curacao, where we spent one week each relaxing before returning home.

The nicest experience of this tour was making of friends with many local families and fellow travelers. Our visitor's book has more than 180 entries, topped off with a sketch of Edith done by Brazil's well-known painter Scliar.

The total car repair and service bill excluding tire service was $187—for seven months and 27,888 miles travel. The continuous life in the VW camper was exceptionally comfortable. We plan to keep the camper for our next trip to Bolivia—Brazil later this year. •

CONTINUED FROM PAGE 67

you can live in it as you drive. This is not a camper that merely goes along for the ride, it works all the way. You can even cook while driving though I, for one, would not care to juggle a hot pot on a bouncing stove, but Mrs. Oster has mastered this art. A thin sheet of sponge rubber on the table top keeps plates from sliding around during meals.

Canned goods shelved on the doors are retained by brackets along the edges of each shelf like those on a boat.

One particularly clever gimmick has been adapted from the cardboard boxes used to carry drinks at drive-in theaters. This is simply a box with round holes to support a glass, a coffee cup, or a bottle of soda cut in the top. When not in use it slides into an under-dash rack, but when you want it you can set it neatly into a fenced-in flat area between the seats. The fence keeps the box in place when you're using it. The box and its mounting are beautifully made and neatly finished in formica so spilled food can simply be washed off. While this is the deluxe way to do this job, the idea could be used in less fancy materials in almost any car. All it would take would be some simple work with plywood to build the box and make some kind of a temporary platform on which to place it for use. When not in use it could be tucked away in a corner out of the way.

It is ideas like this that make Dean Oster's bus so impressive. Every corner has some use and every use is both clever and worthwhile. Seeing a vehicle like his on display is one of the prime attractions of the VWCA Convention. While you or I may never decide to build ourselves a special $10,000 camper bus, we just might get around to adapting one or more of his clever ideas to our own use. And isn't this one reason why you go to a car club convention in the first place? ●

LEFT: All the comforts of home include stove, refrigerator, sink, and full bathroom facilities including shower.

LEFT: Ready for the day, bedding fits in space over engine with flares and fire extinguisher on the side.

Leisure motorist

Motor caravan test

Danbury Multicar

A practical conversion of the compact, economical Volkswagen 216 delivery van powered by a rear-mounted 1493 c.c. air-cooled flat-four. Variety of basic layouts offered to seat up to eight and sleep up to seven (three of them adults). Costs £983 basically; £1,026 10s as tested. Made by Danbury Conversions Limited, Danbury, near Chelmsford, Essex.
Length of test—1,500 miles.

General layout

The Danbury Multicar is one of the smaller vehicles to be converted into a motor caravan, but it makes a thoroughly practical holiday home due largely to the wide-opening double doors on each side and an interior design which allows most of the units comprising the conversion to be shifted around to suit the requirements of the user; there are even alternative waste pipes for the sink to allow for this.

In the basic form, the VW-based Multicar will sleep two adults and two children; one child on the front seats, the other above the rear engine bay; the adults occupy the centrally placed 6 ft. x 4 ft. berth. Folding bunks are extras and provide room for two small children on a 3 ft. 8 in. x 3 ft. 2 in. bed *above* the front seats, and for one adult on a 6 ft. 1 in. x 2 ft. bunk high up on the off-side.

Performance

(Load equivalent to four passengers. Strong wind blowing)
Comfortable cruising speed: 60 m.p.h.
Top speed (banked circuit): 64.2 m.p.h. *
Acceleration, 0-50 through gears: 22.4 sec. *
Standing ¼ mile: 25.0 sec. *
30-50 in top: 18.5 sec.
Hill starting: 1 in 4 gradient: Handbrake held, restart accomplished.
            1 in 3 gradient: Handbrake held, restart accomplished.
Fuel consumption on tour: 29.2 m.p.g.
Speedometer 5% fast; mileage recorder ½% slow.
*Engine governor in operation.

Specification

Length: 14 ft. 0½ in. **Width:** 5 ft. 9 in.
Height: 6 ft. 5 in.
Ground clearance: 9¼ in.
Turning circle: 39 ft. **Fuel capacity:** 8.8 gal.
Engine: 1493 c.c. air-cooled flat-four. 53 b.h.p.
Transmission: Four speed all-synchromesh
Tyres: 7.00 x 14
Extras offered: Webster elevating roof: £79
            Two colours: £20*
            Extra storage unit: £5 15s.*
            Canopy for side doors: £4 16s.*
            Front bunk: £8 18s.*
            Side bunk: £11 10s.
            Side tent: £14 15s.
            Reversing light: £4 10s. *
            Refrigerator: £33 2s. 8d.
            Towing attachment: £11 10s.

*Fitted to test vehicle.

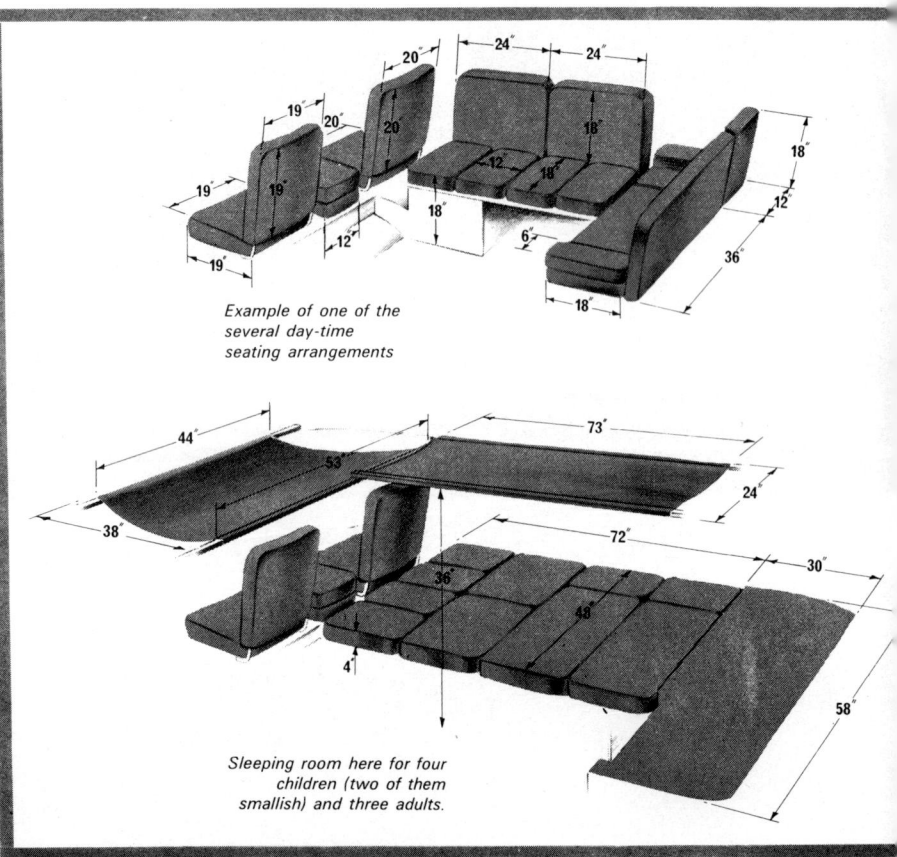

Example of one of the several day-time seating arrangements

Sleeping room here for four children (two of them smallish) and three adults.

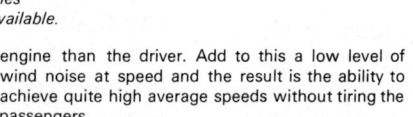

There are double-opening doors at each side. With this simple canopy in position fine-weather catering becomes pleasurable. A larger, pole-supported canopy is also available.

It is best to sit down to the chores and the unit construction layout makes this easy to arrange.

Adults are unable to stand up straight in the van (headroom is 4 ft. 6 in.) but the optional extra Webster elevating roof gives over 6 ft. 5 in.

If the side-mounted tent is taken as an extra, the capacity of the outfit as a holiday home is sufficient for the largest family.

On the road

The Volkswagen van is long in proportion to its width and, initially, the car driver finds there is more behind him than he imagines, so sharp corners have to be taken wide.

The driving position is comfortable; the pedals are easily operated, the gear lever is simple to reach and the almost horizontal steering wheel is of exceptionally large diameter so that the driver, with hands at ten-to-two, finds it comfortable to rest his forearms on the rim. The driving seat leaves one uncramped after a 300-mile run, and the only unnatural movement necessary when driving is the stretch forward to reach the centrally mounted hand brake; in fact, if safety harness is worn, that for the driver would have to be of the inertia reel type to enable him to reach the brake.

The most endearing feature of the vehicle is its ability to cruise at near its top speed without undue mechanical noise. Even passengers in the body of the van are no more conscious of the rear mounted engine than the driver. Add to this a low level of wind noise at speed and the result is the ability to achieve quite high average speeds without tiring the passengers.

There is, incidentally, a governing device on the carburetter which prevents the throttle being opened sufficiently to produce peak engine speeds and this must account for the surprisingly good fuel consumption figure of 29.2 m.p.g. which we achieved; the VW van is perfectly happy on 2-star (minimum 90 octane) petrol. In practice, the governor can be an embarrassment when it causes a sudden cessation of power build-up when passing another vehicle in an intermediate gear.

The Multicar is a vehicle that gives confidence to the driver; this stems partly from the high driving position and partly from the precise handling which allows the van to be positioned accurately and held easily on a chosen course. Strong side winds had no more than an average effect and the few swerves were easily corrected.

The suspension deals well with everything but waves on the road surface; a minor undulation taken at speed will cause the van to pitch markedly, but damping is effective. This pitching is most evident to the driver; those sitting in amidships are less conscious of it.

Roads that are merely rough can be taken fast without risk of the vehicle veering off its course, and in these conditions the whole thing turned out to be rattle-free.

The brakes were powerful and virtually fade-free during 10 successive applications from 60 m.p.h. over 10 miles, the final application being accomplished with hands off the steering wheel (not on a public road).

We were particularly impressed by the Multicar's ability to stop and restart on a 1-in-3 incline, although this was a difficult operation because of the positioning of the handbrake.

Seating and sleeping

There are various seating arrangements possible by ringing the changes with the various movable units—the sink and the storage units—and fitting the cushions into the required positions. The top sketch on the opposite page shows one convenient travelling arrangement and it is possible to seat up to seven adults around the large free-standing table provided.

At night, cushions of various dimensions are rearranged as shown in the lower sketch opposite: the bunk on the right is, in fact, on the rear shelf over the engine bay. In practice, we found that a 10-year-old boy slept comfortably in the bunk *above* the front seats, and the makers assure us that this 38-inch wide bed can be occupied by two smaller children. The rear bunk over the engine bay also proved acceptable to another child. The cushions make a comfortable mattress; one side of them is cloth-covered the other leathercloth and we found it best to use the leather side upwards during the daytime in the interests of cleanliness.

Storage

There is considerable space for bedding, cooking utensils and clothing in the Multicar. Apart from a small wardrobe (24 in. across by 34 in. tall and varying between 10 in. and 18 in. deep), the several storage boxes under the seats take all the bedding one could wish to carry. There are other storage units for crockery and cutlery and a small roof locker, which we found rather prone to condensation. Except when we ate outside beneath the canopy, we used the trays forming the tops of the under-seat storage boxes to serve meals on rather than erecting the table.

Living in it

We started off feeling rather cramped in the Multicar, but as we got the hang of the movable units, it turned out to be quite spacious, even under bad weather conditions. In fine weather, with the canopy over the double doors at one side, it was a very pleasant way to live. The two-burner-and-grill cooker was satisfactory in operation but in bad weather when the doors were shut up, the atmosphere became somewhat oppressive and condensation heavy on metal fittings.

At night with the temperature below freezing, the van was reasonably warm although we were glad of sleeping bags; there is foam insulation behind the roof lining and the interior is lined with Vynide over a soft foam backing. One advantage of the unitary construction of the interior was that it was a simple task to remove all the units to give the interior a quick brush out.

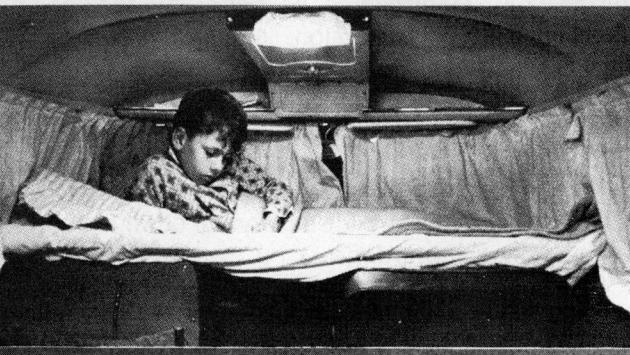

When the van was closed we found it convenient to eat off trays (the storage-unit lids) or off other flat surfaces.

Forward bunk over the front seats. Curtains on runners totally cover the windows at night.

THIS TRANSPORTER IS

NO MORE PUSSYFOOTING FOR THIS VW TRANSPORTER; A NEW ENGINE MADE IT A REAL WILDCAT

By ALEX WALORDY ■ Picture a mild looking blue Volks Transporter that is in dire need of a paint job. Only instead of being barely able to get out of its own way, this beast is doing a fine job of passing Chevies and Fords an gets around trucks in style. We want you to know that this is not a pipe dream, but an actual, dramatic reality.

From the day we got our Volks camper, most road miles were spent plotting and scheming the installation of a large sized American V8, carefully concealed within the confines of the body. Some of the ideas were probably in the realm of feasibility, like mounting the Camper body on top of an American chassis, or placing that V8 behind the driver's seat, but all of them involved an objectionable amount of money, time and effort.

Other schemes were time-proven, though not always successful, like installing a Porsche engine (pretty good) or a Corvair engine—not really noted for its durability. The eye opener came during VW's showing of its 68's. In fact, a ride in the new bus proved that this big box on wheels can be made to move out. What's more, the engine of the new bus produces against the odds of increased weight

Out comes old engine as a unit to make room for the new.

and frontal area. Why not a new bus engine for our camper. In fact, better yet, why not a new 1600 engine? That extra 100 cubic centimeters doesn't really tell the full story. It's the impact of the two carburetors, bigger valves and other similar amenities which add up to pretty nice performance in Squarebacks and Fastbacks.

A few phone calls quickly established that 1500 Transporter engines weren't appreciably cheaper than the 1600, and, actually, much scarcer. The price range turned out to be between $200 and $300, and the low bidder proved to be a chap named Ziggy, who presides over a few acres of imported machinery out in College Point, New York.

Ziggy proved to be a gold mine of information on the subject of VW engine swaps and informed us that a six spring clutch and small disc used with 40 horse engines just wouldn't cut the mustard. What was needed, according to Ziggy, was a bigger disc, a nine spring clutch plate of a type used with the bigger engine and a 1500 Transporter flywheel. The 1600 one will not mesh with an old style starter.

After acquiring our Volks bus we had gone through a short period of trial and tribulation, while seeking out a service place. The ones closer to home proved a bit unimaginative, but in Hempstead, Long Island, we hit pay dirt in the form of Art Echtle, a live wire service manager who makes appointments for the next day instead of the following week, and who has a pretty fair idea of how to cram a few extra hours into a day on short notice.

Naturally, before buying the engine we consulted with him and got quite a detailed explanation of why a 1500 would be better for the job, a simple bolt on conversion. "With a 1600 you'll spend a day and a half in the shop tending to a million details", Art Echtle warned us. He also added that the shop had done one installation of the type, and had nothing but problems. However, hearing that the job had been accomplished pretty much clinched matters for us, and all other advice was blithely disregarded.

We must admit that Arthur wasn't wrong, and the time spent was 20 hours, or two and a half days, but this involved much extraneous work and some

A TIGER!

The engine compartment takes on a new appearance with the 1600 engine, and individual parts are more easily accessible.

unexpected difficulties. We ran into things like a missing throttle arm that had to be made up overnight because ordering one would have taken a week. The throttle shafts were frozen solid, and it took a major engineering effort to free them up. Buy new ones? From whom?

There was also a wide range of "may-as-well-while-the engine-is-out" jobs. This included generator brushes, plugs, points, and a host of other piddly time-consuming details. Finally, we had our own ideas on how the detailing should be done, and so the hours built up. On a straight-through basic, with what we know now, a day would probably turn the trick, with all parts lined up in advance.

No one will ever accuse the crew at "Small Cars" of being mere parts replacers. In fact, the project became something of a shop pet and advice flowed freely, most of it good and very much

to the point. Ewald Hagen, the shop foreman, took a paternal interest in the engine change, and Cliff Chandler, the man who did the actual wrench turning, proved to be an ingenious self-starter, and mighty handy with torch and welding rod.

The 1600 engine is both wider and longer than a 1300, and fitting its 35½ inch wing span into the 29½ inch space available in the stock Transporter called for quite a bit of head scratching. We did manage to carefully avoid cutting into structural parts like the two frame rails which extend back to the rear bumper. Trimming some of the sheet metal at the sides of the engine compartment and on the engine cowling proved sufficient, for snaking in the engine during the preliminary fitting. Most cuts were made with a cold chisel rather than with a cutting torch to avoid jagged edges, and burned-off paint. The only place where a cutting torch became unavoidable was at the rear corners

Oil filler pipe is short Chevy pipe welded to the VW pipe.

Cold cutting with a chisel takes longer, but the job is neat.

Tail pipe is welded to adapter flap and also to the muffler.

Completed muffler fits neatly within stock bumper location.

THIS TRANSPORTER IS A TIGER!

where some clearance was needed for the air duct elbows. Even now, the only way to install the engine is to temporarily remove those elbows.

In their quest for trunk space, the Wolfsburg engineers came up with a clever design that relocates the fan from the top of the engine on back to the rear, at the end of the crankshaft. With typical Teutonic precision, they then proceeded to add an elaborate fan shroud that sticks out behind the engine and leads to a dust-free rubber connection and to ducts which are wrapped around the rear of the car. This results in a clean air supply piped in from the sides of the fenders.

Unfortunately, the old style Transporter just doesn't offer room for these niceties. Even worse, shutting the engine compartment lid effectively seals the front of the fan shroud, and cuts off the supply of cooling air. Taking a pair of snips to the front of this fancy housing and cutting off most of it gained air passage space all around. The bottom end of the housing was heated to a dull red with a torch and reshaped to form a tight fit against the muffler in an effort to keep road dirt from reaching the fan.

Attempts at cutting down the panel under the engine compartment door so that it wouldn't interfere with the big 1600 muffler and fan ended in dismal failure, because by the time all the openings were cut, little of its mechanical strength was left. The final outcome was to simply leave it off, which saved a few pounds and helped compensate for the extra 60 pounds of engine weight. The muffler comes up high and has a protective shield above it which we simply painted black as a temporary expedient. Later a small aluminum vanity shield will be added to fill the space between the

Sheet metal sides of engine compartment had to be trimmed.

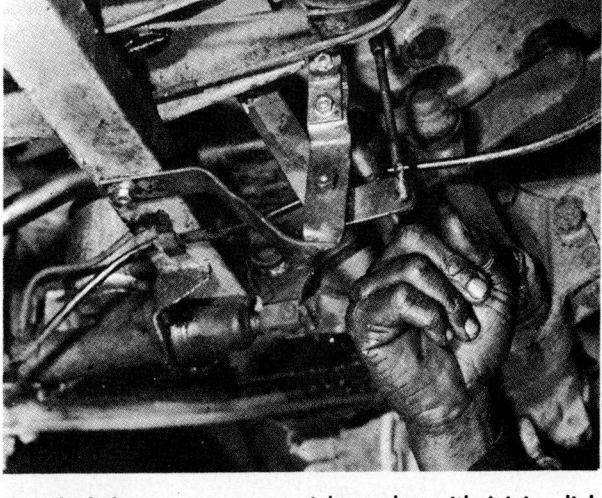
Throttle linkage arms are at right angles with joining link.

Stock flywheel was replaced with one from 1500 Transporter.

The 1600 engine, wider than a 1300, required body trimming.

bumper and the engine lid.

We spent considerable time on the accelerator linkage, working it out until it became smooth and letter perfect. Nothing can ruin an engine conversion as quickly as a throttle that sticks, doesn't open all the way or has a harsh initial opening. A quick check of the possibilities showed that the basic linkage of the 1600 is excellent, with two individually adjustable connecting rods leading to each carb from a central arm which in turn links up with the cable that leads from the accelerator.

All adjustments were made right from scratch, beginning with the throttle levers. We began making all the adjustments right from scratch by first disconnecting each throttle lever from its rod and return spring. The idle speed is first turned all the way out until the throttle seats fully, then turned back in ¾ of a turn to provide the base idle speed setting. Next the short connecting rods at each carb were adjusted to give a favorable angle of attack against the relay arms, and the individual return springs were hooked up. Finally, the long connecting rods were set to fit freely on each carburetor. By working back from the carburetors, we insured an even linkage setting which would not interfere with a quick return to idle. A rod and lever linkage works best when the two are at right angles to each other. If you set up the linkage so this occurs approximately at the mid point of the available travel, you'll avoid excess angling, and over center action where the throttle can hang up.

On a stock 1300 engine the cable control is guided by a long tube that passes through the fanhousing. The 1600 engine has a somewhat different arrangement which would have left our

CONTINUED ON PAGE 90

If you look closely, you can see that the roof extension is made from a hunk of Kombi in front joined to a bit of Microbus at the rear.

4WD, TWIN-ENGINED VW CAMPER

by Jon and Anne Skelly

$600 for parts plus priceless ingenuity create a VW camper unlike any to ever come out of Wolfsburg.

Very bizarre but very practical is this camper built by Dwain Schenck of West Carrolton, Ohio. Started as a spare-time project in 1963, it now boasts sleeping space for seven, its own water supply, propane heat, a 4-wheel drive utilizing two engines and an amazingly low dollar investment.

Dwain's inspiration for this unique and uncommonly useful vehicle came from his hobby of camping and his need to locate a camper large enough to accommodate his active family of seven. Unable to find a commercial camper

suitable, Dwain created his own model. The result is the biggest attention-getter in the Dayton area since Barnum.

Few people who come to stare realize the variety of parts used to make up the camper. Dwain owns and operates a body shop which does a big percentage of the Volkswagen body work in the Dayton area and has an inside track on VW salvage parts. Many observers mistake the basic unit for a Kombi, but hard-core Volkswagen fans may note the door on the left side and correctly recognize it as a delivery van. Dwain

purchased it for a paltry $200 from a local Volkswagen dealer. The second drive unit became available as scrap after an identical truck came out the loser in a disagreement with some unnamed object. Here the investment was only $37.50. A Kombi supplied the front portion of the raised roof and cost $25. The rear portion of the top is from a Microbus that met an immovable object and was acquired for $20. All these ingredients plus more hours than Dwain cares to remember make for an interesting creation. Also included with

88

The sight of Schenck's camper coming down the highway has been known to make some people take the pledge. Spare is outside for the usual reasons of room.

Set up for the night, the camper is almost as large and fully as private as the average motel room and amortized over the years, a lot cheaper.

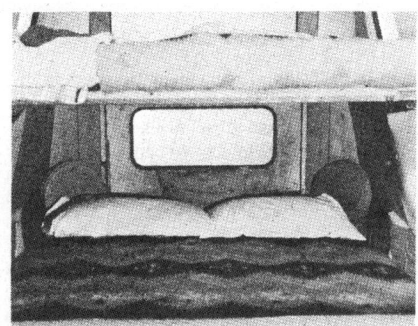

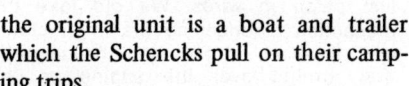

Length of the camper permits permanent two-decker beds with more headroom for the top one than will be found in current commercially-made extensions.

Builder Schenck relaxes in his creation. Mounting wash basin on top of heater (right) not only humidifies the air but gives fairly instant hot water.

the original unit is a boat and trailer which the Schencks pull on their camping trips.

All together, what does a bus like this cost? If you can do the body work, find a used delivery van at rock-bottom price and purchase the rest at salvage, you might be able to do it for only $600 as Dwain did although this figure, of course, does not include labor.

The interior is paneled and a set of snap-on terrycloth curtains cover the windows from front to rear when camping. A propane heater which came from a trailer and cost $40 provides year-round comfort. As an added touch, a wash basin was installed in the top of the heater and a drain was run to the outside, all of which amounts to an ingenious method to provide hot water and to humidify the air. Front mounting of the spare tire gives added space inside. There are three dome lights for extra illumination and a complement of folding chairs, stored behind the driver's

seat, to make the "living room" useful at night. Carpet covers the floor area which is ideal for the smaller children to play on in transit. The full-size bunk beds wouldn't cramp a party of Watusi warriors, and make no concessions to comfort. They occupy the space behind the bench seat and require no preparation.

The vehicle invariably draws many onlookers when parked and the most common question is always whether or not it has 4-wheel drive. It not only has 4-wheel drive but two complete engines,

two transmissions and even two batteries. There is nothing mysterious about the twin-engine, 4-wheel drive arrangement. Since the VW contains all its power and power transmission components neatly arranged about the rear axle, you simply weld on another identical unit. To the average person, doing this would be about as simple as Chinese arithmetic, but to Dwain, it was easy.

The transmission shifting linkage between the units is simple, but Dwain reports that it was the hardest part of the conversion to develop. This linkage can be disconnected in 30 minutes and allows the camper to run on either engine. A mechanism is in the works which will allow this operation to be performed from the driver's seat.

Rear clutch operation is via a second cable which runs through a length of electrical conduit. Throttle linkage to the rear is accomplished by a discarded choke cable. Access to the top of the front engine is through a panel under the bed.

The only difference in the controls at the driver's seat is the addition of one ignition-starter switch unit. The bus drives well and other than a slightly enlarged turning circle, no handling problems have been encountered. The same features that make it an ideal camper also combine to make it an ideal highway cruising bus. Being able to stand upright or to lie down helps passengers overcome the boredom and physical discomfort usually encountered on long trips, and greatly increases the feasibility of non-stop trips in which the drivers relieve each other.

This feature proved its worth when Dwain and two friends attended the Daytona 500, driving the camper on the approximately 2000-mile round trip. The outing turned into a personal-appearance tour for the camper, which was the star of the show at every stop as well as on the highway. Dwain was kept busy explaining its origin and capabilities. The men alternated driving stints and kept moving at 60 to 65 mph all the way.

Camping or cruising, you'll seldom see the equal of this rig, which combines the best qualities of Volkswagen, Greyhound and the Superchief. ●

TIGER

CONTINUED FROM PAGE 87

control wire grating against a small opening in the sheet metal. so we added an extra VW rod, plus a 1600 link, to keep things moving smoothly, and to avoid having the cable act at an odd angle. Liberal amounts of graphite powder were squirted into the cable housing to keep it working freely.

Had we hooked up the Transporter cable to the accelerator linkage and let it go at that, the throttles would have never opened more than two thirds of the way, with a corresponding loss of power. Even a stock Transporter is pretty marginal in this respect. Leverage was traded for extra travel, by lengthening the cable side of an "L" shaped rod. In actual practice, this called for making up a new pivot bracket, a new arm, and a longer link from the accelerator pedal to the "L," since the stock design didn't allow enough room. A little hammering on the sheet metal which encloses the undersides up front bumped it out enough to clear the new gadgetry.

Even a simple matter like giving the engine an occasional drink of oil turned out to be a problem. On a 1600 Squareback, or a Fastback, the oil filler is inside the car. Elaborate leak-proofing precautions were taken by the factory in form of a section fixed to the body and connected to the engine via flexible rubber coupling. Even the combination oil filler cap and dip stick is an ingenious contraption with a mystery slide-in tip. It's all great, except that there was no room for this on the Transporter.

The air inlet breather cap of the 1600 could have been used for an oil fill, but we were strongly advised against this by all parties concerned. Point is that a small screen under this breather is used to trap airborne dirt particles before they reach the engine. Pouring in oil through that screen would automatically wash down any dirt trapped there.

We took off on a fruitless search at parts departments at nearby American dealerships but found out that no one stocks oil filler pipes because most V8's have the oil cap right on the rocker covers. Fortunately, the small Chevy V8 is an exception. Its short filler pipe even necks down to form a perfect fit around the oil filler tube bolted to the Volks engine. The Volkswagen boys simply welded up a VW-Chevy assembly and they also heated and twisted the Volkswagen pipe a few degrees toward the engine, giving us room to close the engine lid. As a finishing touch, a small tube was welded to the top of the breather pipe, allowing us to insert a Ford dipstick so that the oil can be checked without pulling the filler cap. Incidentally, after several hundred miles of operation the engine is still bone-dry and leak free. The resonator on a stock 1600 is placed behind the muffler which would have forced us to move the bumper back out of the way. The Volks boys solved the problem by doing away with the resonator altogether. An odd section of 60 Buick cross-over pipe was welded in under the muffler, fastened section of 60 Buick cross-over pipe was and works just fine. The new and throatier sound adds driving pleasure without calling attention to the car.

One incidental benefit of the 1600 is instant car heat, something the old bus never had. Admittedly, we worked for it. Outlets and connecting hoses of a 1600 are larger than the ones on the '61 Transporter. This is readily solved by either using a reducing adapter or two hoses taped one inside the other. Two small extra 1600 heater outlets which lead to the rear of the car were simply pinched together and welded shut. The heater control cables were detached from their brackets at the rear of the bus and moved up to connect with the 1600 heater arms on the engine.

Among other details, the voltage regulator is now mounted off to one side instead of on the generator and the boys from Small Cars added a complete new electrical harness at the rear, rather than just patch in wires. We did take the precaution of checking the fit of clutch and flywheel in the bell housing by first turning over the engine on the starter, and with the coil wire pulled out—so the engine wouldn't start. No scraping sounds came from the bell housing, and everything proved OK but on some of the older models a little hand grinding is necessary.

Last item on the agenda was to add a couple of spring clips for shutting the engine lid. There is enough clearance between the lid and the front of the fan to provide air passage for cooling. However, we prefer to run with the lid spaced further out away from its closed position, especially for long high speed hauls in hot weather. This preserves a fully stock sleeper appearance and helps us net those surprised looks from other "we-have-been-passed-again" bus owners. . ●

AMERICAN ADS THAT SELL VW COMMERCIALS

Who dunks trucks? Volkswagen.

How much longer can it stay in business?

CLEVER advertising helps to sell Volkswagens all over the world. Especially in America. Reproduced on this page, from "Volkswagen Nine Lives Later" **(by Dan R. Post, marketed in the United Kingdom by Vivian Gray, Hurstpierpoint)** are five typical, brilliant ads that have helped to sell the VW commercial in the US.

The lighthearted blurb that accompanies each ad makes fascinating, convincing reading. How do you use a picture of a bicycle to sell a car? The bicycle ad blurb begins: "The delivery bicycle was a great time and money saver in its day . . ." And ends: "Besides, where can you find room on a bicycle for your company name and phone number in letters a foot high?"

And in case you're wondering why Volkswagen trucks get dunked the blurb for this ad explains: "Every VW truck body gets dunked in a vat of special rust resistant primer. Not sprayed. Not splashed. Submerged . . ." And so on.

Ads like these give VW dealers a flying start to their huge sales of VW commercial vehicles in America.

Volkswagen, the truck that picks up more for less

Who puts raincoats on pick-ups? Volkswagen

You can save enough running a Volkswagen Truck to buy yourself a Volkswagen Sedan

INSULATE YOUR VW BUS

BY ERNEST E. HICKMAN

▶ You can buy more warmth and quiet for your Volkswagen bus if you're willing to spend some time and a few—even a very few—dollars. What you get is insulation, and you can have as little or as much of it as you want to suit whatever time or money you want to spend. For while the VW bus may be the greatest box on wheels in the whole world, it probably also is the coldest and noisiest, and least-insulated, too.

The floors are probably the best place to add insulation; they transmit the most road noise. But if you plan to insulate the walls, too, better do that first. Otherwise, the floor insulation may get in the way of the wall panels. The ceiling you probably can forget about; it already contains most of the insulation in the bus, and adding more would be an extremely difficult undertaking.

Assuming that you're going to do the whole job (floors and walls), start it by removing the spare tire and all the seats. The front ones lift out readily; the back ones are a little trickier. After pulling off the kick panel in front of the rear seat bench, remove the two anchor bolts and then lift and pull the seat bench out of its position behind the heater outlet. With the bench removed, and the two anchoring machine bolts at the back taken out, the seat back

can be removed by lifting it straight up to clear the armrests, then pulling it forward and out.

Next comes the wall panel removal. A power or spring-return screwdriver will help with the job, because it entails removing and replacing several dozen slot-head sheet-metal screws. In addition, the latch handles on the front doors will have to be removed. This is accomplished by depressing the plastic escutcheon plates against the door to expose the retaining pin in the handle base. This pin can be driven out of the handle with a $\frac{3}{32}$″ pin punch or other tool. A helper will be valuable here to depress the escutcheon while you remove the pin.

Panels bearing arm rests can be removed by raising them straight up; this lifts the armrest backing plates off the hooks on the bus wall.

Baring the interior of the bus this way offers a rare opportunity to wirebrush any rust spots you may find, and to check the condition of the sheet drains and vents. If it's available, a small, cup-type wire brush chucked into an electric drill will make the cleanup job a lot easier.

When the wirebrushing is done, take time to vacuum the entire interior of the bus; insulation adhesive won't stick to dirt, nor will masking tape. And masking off all the exposed upholstery is the next step. Newspapers will prove useful for this job, provided they're applied several layers thick. The areas closest to the floor deserve the most attention, because this is where the spatters and fog will fall. And while you have the tape out, use small pieces of it to keep the condensation drains in the wall ribs from being clogged by cement or undercoating.

While the walls are dry and clean, hold the insulation in place and cut it to fit. Then arrange the pre-cut pieces in sequence so that you'll be able to fit them in place at the first try; once the adhesive is in place, where the insulation touches, it stays.

Now, while the masking is in place and the insulation pre-cut, apply anti-rust primer or push-button undercoat to the wire-brushed areas. If necessary, let this dry before applying adhesive liberally to the areas to be insulated. Keep the

RIGHT: Areas to be insulated should be wire brushed and coated with anti-rust primer before applying the adhesive. Apply adhesive liberally and allow it to dry.

cement off the places where the upholstery panels will rest; there's no point in cementing those in place. And either be equally careful around the door latches, or mask them, too.

When the adhesive is dry enough to be tacky, fit the pre-cut insulation batts in place, pressing each one firmly into the adhesive—and pressing every square inch of it. If you're using glass-fiber insulation, be sure to wear gloves. Otherwise, your hands may absorb an uncomfortable lot of tiny glass splinters.

While the side panels are removed from the rear luggage deck, plan your method of insulating its floor. You can put a layer of carpet padding or similar insulation beneath the floor carpet, or you can lay carpeting on top of the original floor covering, or you can lay a felt-backed rubber mat on top of the existing pad. More than likely, the use of carpet will prove most effective and by far the easiest. It can be done after the sidewall panels are in place, too.

If, however, you plan to cement carpet padding directly to the metal floor, trim it with a half-inch margin around the edge so that the original deck cover will have room to fold over the pad and fit beneath the sidewall panels as it did originally.

The passenger compartment floor offers the same choice of insulating methods. The selection depends primarily on the use to which you put your bus and whether you prefer the smooth surface of the original rubber mat or the softness of carpet. For the maximum insulation, use some of the new indoor-outdoor carpeting over a thick felt carpet pad. You can anchor this thick sandwich in place with a few well-placed oval-head sheet metal screws and washers. You can screw a tackless aluminum edgebinder across the door threshold in the same way the binder is used in a home or office.

Or, if you'd prefer to be able to remove the carpet for laundering, you will find that the washable carpet sold for use in bathrooms can be had in sizes approximating bus floor sizes. While not such effective

carpet-plus-padding system can be used here, too, if provision is made for pedal clearance. Use the original rubber mat as a pattern for cutting the indoor-outdoor carpet. The edges of this material can be left unbound without deteriorating.

While cementing the underlayment to the floors might hold it more firmly and deaden sound more effectively, it might also encourage corrosion by trapping water. Leaving the carpet loose allows some ventilation and permits easier evaporation.

Of course, you can deter floor corrosion by applying extra paint before insulating. There are many good rust-inhibiting paints available, including those used to coat the inside of metal eavestrough gutters.

Ordinary roof-patching cements can be used either as undercoating or as insulation adhesive, too. Basically, these are solutions of asphalt in volatile solvents. Some have asbestos or glass fiber fillers; some also are quite flammable. Some are so thick they must be applied with a trowel; these are best for undercoating, since they deaden sound when applied thickly. Others—even after thorough stirring—are thin enough to brush on. These are best for attaching pads; simply apply the cement, let it dry until tacky, and press the pad in place.

The pad itself can be either glass fiber or felt matting; carpet underlayment works well, too. Either ½" or 1" glass fiber blanket can be used; these are thicknesses commonly found in lumberyards and hard-

ware stores. Depending on how well you fit it, about 50 square feet of insulation will be needed to complete the side insulation of a VW bus. Kits containing this much glass fiber blanket and the cement to install it are available by mail, too. J. C. Whitney, 1917-19 Archer Avenue, Chicago, Illinois 60616, carries these kits in half and full-inch thicknesses, for $6.50 and $8.95, respectively. (It's their catalog numbers 14-189 and 14-188.)

(J. C. Whitney also sells jute carpet underpadding, a yard wide and two yards long, for $2.79.)

If you'd like to cut the cost of your bus insulation to the very bone, try scrounging carpet padding scraps from a carpet layer. His snips and bits are completely adequate for your purposes—big sheets have to be cut into little pieces to make them fit, anyhow.

If, after you've insulated the interior of the bus, you'd still like a little more warmth, try insulating the underfloor duct that runs forward from the engine. While a completely miserable job, especially in drippy weather, wrapping this duct with pipe insulation and vapor-proof tape will increase the delivery of warm air to the front of the bus.

But whether you take this step or not, you'll find your insulated bus is far more satisfying to ride in. Damping reverberations in those slab sides, and blocking some of the road noise from the floor will make the ride much quieter. And instead of clanging, the doors close with a solid "thud." ●

RIGHT: All the required insulating strips should be cut to fit before the adhesive is applied. Insulation is applied when the adhesive is dry enough to become tacky.

VOLKSWAGEN DOESN'T
UNDERSTAND IT, USED
CAR DEALERS HAVEN'T
A CLUE, EVEN LLOYD
BODINE IS MYSTIFIED,
SO WE WENT TO AN
EXPERT TO EXPLAIN THE
BUS PHENOMENON

VOLKSWAGEN MICROBUS

VIEWPOINT: TOM FINN

● *Because of the VW Microbus' popularity among young people and the so-called militant left, we thought it reasonable to get a spokesman of that particular group to explain his views. Our choice is Tom Finn, a 22-year-old former college student who is now the co-chairman of the Leon Trotsky Socialist Purge Committee presently headquartered in San Gabriel, California. Finn gained his first bit of notoriety when he was arrested for picketing the grave of Albert Schweitzer, whom he claimed was "an imperialist war monger." He has been active in the Columbia, Berkeley and San Francisco State campus disturbances and is presently heading a committee to assist Jerry Rubin and Bobby Seale to purchase a home in Federal Judge Julius J. Hoffman's neighborhood. Described by some as among the more militant of the young political activists, Finn recently denounced the SDS as "a pitiful gang of capitalist pawns" and claims members of the Weathermen faction of the party are "pansies." The son of a well-to-do insurance executive in Shaker Heights, Ohio, Finn has used his bus to travel across the country, attending political meetings and the rock festivals at Woodstock, New York and Altamont, California. After persistent questioning, he admitted his daddy bought him the VW on his 17th birthday.—Ed.*

Before we get into it, I'd like to apologize to all my brothers in the Movement to free the world from the grip of the imperialist warmongers for my being conned into writing for this fascist-racist pig magazine. I mean, at first it seems weird, me being so heavy with Peace and Understanding and then showing up in the middle of these lowly dupes of scumbag capitalism. Bad vibes. I know it, but then I figured if these establishment creeps were dumb enough to let a little truth into their materialistic rag, take advantage of it. After all, if they gave me a chance to talk to the board of directors of General Motors or to the genocide merchants who run the pentagon and the Red Cross, I'd do it, so why not one of their propaganda sheets like *Car and Driver?*

So all you straights out there want to know how we use that machine to advance our groovy, gentle life style? How can I tell you? What is there to say to dupes like you? In fact, until you stop the genocide in Berkeley, not to mention Viet Nam, your heads will be so clouded with hate that I can't give you any help at all. But, because I am dedicating my life to bringing Peace and Gentleness to the earth, I will try to be mellow. It won't do any good and we'll probably have to kill all of you sooner or later, but no fascist pig is ever going to die saying I didn't try to rap with him.

Like the VW bus is the freakiest car on the scene. Mine is a 1965 model Microbus—the heaviest. That was before they changed to the flash model, with all the bourgeois styling and decadent mechanical improvements. The new buses are real bummers, but my '65 is so spaced out you wouldn't believe it. I mean, I see you guys making it down the freeway in your bucks giving me the shakes and when you pass me and my bus, and then telling your old lady and your kids in their little boy scouts army suits to "look at the freaks in the VW bus." You will never dig it, and that's why we're going to have to run the new world without you. I mean, man, if there was a way of convincing you what a bum trip the united states is on right now, you might have a chance, but no way. Lee Roi Jones said, "Burn, Baby, Burn," and that's what's going to happen to you heel clickers out there on your smog-choked freeways when the Revolution comes, led by all the heads and the crazies and the speed freaks and Mick Jagger and Sonny Barger and guys who realize that your world is bullshit and violence. Sure, Sonny and his Angels have been known to hassle a few guys in their time, but I happen to be one of their staunchest defenders. Like at that beautiful, freaky Altamont concert. Sure, the Angels had to kill a guy, and a lot of straights said it was a bad scene the way we all talk about Peace and then let the Angels kill a guy while the Stones are freaking out everybody with "Sympathy for the Devil." But is that as bad as My Lai or all those other imperialist acts of genocide you straights perpetrate every day? After all, the Angels are basically honest. They have a *very* rigid moralistic code. The Stones asked the Angels to come down to guard the stage and those cats did what they asked them to do, and just because they used cut-down pool cues to keep the people away, a lot of cats say it was a bum trip. But is that any worse than the mace or the clubs the pigs use? I mean, let's be reasonable!

What was really beautiful about the Altamont killing is that some film cats got the whole thing with their cameras. I mean I'm hip to basically socialistic, anti-establishment morality plays like *Bonnie and Clyde* and *The Wild Bunch* with their honest displays of violence, and I am really freaked about seeing the real thing. There it will be, in wide-screen, 70 mm, the Angels sawing up that cat who went against their rigid, moralistic code. Far out!

If you give me a choice, I'd rather have the Berdoo Angels hassling me than the pigs. You know, if you've a strict moral code like the Angels, you've got to expect trouble if you violate it. That's what freedom is all about.

I might as well tell you that the pigs busted me at Altamont and it all related to my bus. We were on our way up to the concert from our commune with Shiek, Mona, Fritz, Betsy, Murph and a freaky hitchhiker we picked up who claimed to be a warlock. Now we are on the freeway and have been pretty freaked out because Fritz has been passing around a gallon of Mountain Vin Rose with a couple of "Reds" mixed in. Organic! So anyway, I am grooving along the freeway and I will admit to being pretty zonked—but nothing like the guys and the chicks in the back. Shiek and Mona are balling by the engine, while Murph is reading an astrology table and this freaky witch is showing everybody this groovy goat's head he is carrying around in an old army duffle bag. Suddenly there is this big black and white armored personnel carrier alongside me, forcing the bus onto the shoulder. The pigs from the california highway patrol! Man did they hassle us. Shiek was ready to go after the tall, skinny one with his Bowie knife but he got it caught in his fly and cut himself. Then he was rolling around in the back of the bus with a big hurt noise coming out of him and the pigs were all over me, checking me for tabs and keys. They couldn't find anything, but that didn't stop those police-state stormtroopers from putting a bust on me. And you know for what? For a lousy little infraction like driving the wrong way on the freeway, which you straights do every day in your fat-ass caddies and get away with. So I am stoned and I take an on-ramp backwards in my little bus and the next thing I know I'm being hassled by the pigs. That's your fascist racist america for you!

It's almost as bad everywhere else. I have driven my bus across the country three times and each time Big Brother has hassled me for something. My long hair, my freaky clothes, my parole violations. Once I was busted because the pigs were attracted to my bus because of the peace symbols on the side and then they found my sawed-off 12-gauge Remington some guys in the Hayward Angels had given me to protect myself. I mean man, those guys have a strict moral code and *nobody* hassles them! Those pigs took my 12-gauge away before I had a chance to fight.

The bus is groovy for anarchy too. It holds a mimeograph machine just perfect and we can run through a neighborhood about 40 mph with a couple of cats grinding away on the mimeo with back doors open and it's just like dropping leaflets from an airplane. Freaky!

A Volkswagen bus symbolizes freedom. It is perfectly functional; like it is the young American Revolutionaries' counterpart to the Russian tractor. Sure, a whole lot of fake cop-out types like the surfers and reactionary establishment college skinheads use them. But among us it means truth and commitment and the right to freak out and get away from the uptight racists who run this country. I mean, man,

just give me my bus, a groovy chick, a jug of muscatel and a few Reds and I'll put down vibes you wouldn't believe.

Now a whole lot of straights don't understand the revolutionary-anarchistic-freak-out-head-scene and I'm perfectly willing to acknowledge that, providing they understand that when we take over, they are going to have to change their ways unless they want to get offed like all the cats they offed just because they didn't agree with them! It's only right. Comes the Revolution we'll all be sitting around stoned, plugged into heavy music and taking art in a century-long freak-out. Two-thousand one! Organic!

I'm only hoping my bus lasts. Sure, a lot of cats are driving around in older models and I confess that sometimes this bugs me. After all, when you get off the trip for new things you get conscious about good things like older buses and about how much more meaningful they are. Funny, what a shuck the older generation is, yet how groovy older buses are. It may have something to do with my being a Capricorn. Saturn rules in the Tenth sign of the Zodiac and Capricorn rules the knees. I mean, who needs to know all that bullshit history about decadent western civilization when you can know beautiful things about Capricorn. Celestial.

I had this one bummer with my Volkswagen. One weekend me and a couple of guys split for the desert to rap about the revolution and drop a little acid under the stars. Well what the hell happens but a sandstorm, which woofed and whistled around my bus for about two hours while we were all stoned inside thinking the earth is stopping. What a bum trip! Anyway, when the wind died down, I discovered that it had polished the VW's paintwork like a baby's ass. It looked new! Man, it messed my mind, looking at my old bus

and seeing it shiny like it belonged to some rich establishment kid. At first I thought I'd lay out some bread to have it re-painted, then Fritz says, "We'll paint the freaking thing ourselves!" I told him I didn't want any of that fake psychedelic freakout shit on it because every housewife in sausalito is driving around in a bus painted so it looks like the Merry Pranksters went after it with stencils. *That's a bummer!*

So one sunny afternoon we get Fritz and Betty, Shiek and Mona and Murph and a whole lot of groovy people together with this five-gallon barrel of olive drab military paint somebody got somewhere and freaked out on some "Mother's Little Helper" and a few jugs of vin rose. Broom city! We all got to sloshing around on that VW with these kitchen brooms and before anyone knew it, we'd covered everything, tires, hubcaps, windows, everything. Man, we had good vibes that day. Except we couldn't see where we were going very well with the heavy paint on the windows and the pigs nailed us on the freeway again. What a bummer! Those pigs laid a rap on us for not being able to see out the windows—as if we *wanted* to look at their filthy, despoiled, smog-covered landscape in the first place!

But comes the Revolution and it'll all be different. When the signs are conjuncting right and the vibes are good, someday the straights will hear this low rumble over the hills. It'll be us, the young freak army, descending on them and their split-level racist hell with our painted-out buses and our 12-gauge Remingtons blazing out the windows. Freaky! And Leon Trotsky and Capricorn and all those stoned. . . . Bummers . . . Mao . . . truth . . .

Ed. note: At this point Mr. Finn's handwriting became illegible and subsequent attempts to contact him at his Palm Springs mailing address have brought no result.

CONTINUED FROM PAGE 64
more normal grade fuel than a sedan. Taking the German DIN norms, the sedan is rated at 31.5 mpg and the Kombi at 23.5 while the new van comes in at 30 mpg even. Another plus for small businesses.

With exterior size ever more important in our cities the van's dimensions are important too. Using the same wheelbase as a 1200 KG or sedan, the van is only 5 inches wider than the Beetle but 3 inches narrower than the Kombi. It is 9 inches higher than a sedan of course, though height is less important in traffic, and nearly 8 inches shorter than the Kombi.

But the dimension which counts in parking is overall length and here Westfalia has scored for real. The van is not only a long foot shorter than the Kombi it is even 4 inches shorter than a 1200 sedan, which makes for true compactness. Needless to say, you pay in overall cubic load capacity but the need there depends on what you have to haul. The Kombi is rated at twice the van's 81 cubic feet of load area, and better

than twice its 905-pound load limit above the weight of car and driver.

To clear up a few more statistics since they decide a van buyer: you can carry bamboo poles two inches over five feet without going past the back of the driver's seat. Dispensing with the right-hand seat you could carry even longer items. There are 18 square feet of floor space and the sliding door opening is a respectable 48 x 32 inches, very close to that of the optional Kombi slider. The rear door is over two feet wide and three high.

I mentioned interior length without the second seat—which is the way mini-vans will come normally. The second seat is an option which rather cancels some of the chief benefits. The sliding doors flank the cockpit after all, as they must in so short a vehicle. With a second seat in place you can still walk to the back but have to wiggle past the extra roost.

With just a driving seat the delivery man can pull up, walk to the rear for any small item and step out

the sliding door on either side at curb height. They have achieved a true walk in van (all right you do have to duck a little) covering a minimum road area.

While the cockpit trim is simplicity to the nth degree, your driver has anything necessary, including a fairly upright wheel, but less truck-positioned than in the Kombi, speedometer and reserve tap, plus switches. The floor is wooden slats the seat adjusts both forward, aft and for back rake. You sit fairly upright but that's a good position in tight places. The nose bin has space for the spare wheel, fuel tank and a tool roll if you keep it small.

As a Westfalia rep noted wryly, "it may not be pretty but it is functional," and apparently he had been peeking. Functional, as Webster might say, in the sense of being "designed or developed chiefly from the point of view of use." Wholly and carefully in the case of the Westfalia VW van, which is the nicest thing you can say about any utilitarian vehicle. ●

JON DAHLSTROM ILLUSTRATION

O'KANE & THE ENCHANTED BUS

BY DICK O'KANE

"**Y**OU EVER GET the feeling you're driving around inside a whale?" my wife asked.

That pretty well described it, assuming that the insides of whales also feature acute flatulence along with the dampness, darkness and mud. Rain slashed like birdshot against our great tin container, overwhelming the wipers, which were already having their problems with the wind; in the really bad gusts, they left the windshield to wave vaguely about in the air. Couldn't see a thing past the 20 feet of gloomy dirt road the lights lit up. But we kept lurching and racking slowly onward—sooner or later the road *had* to go up there.

We had been sloshing down a secondary Spanish highway toward Almeria and a place on a beach we know about when we spotted the crumbling ruin on a high pinnacle above a little town. It looked both inviting and forbidding, brooding there in the last light of the stormy day.

"What do you think?" I asked Jeffi. We're both nuts about Moorish ruins. Nobody but *nobody* bothers you when you spend the night camped in one, and there's an odd sort of fascination in sitting there in the moonlight, letting the place's strange, ancient vibrations wash over you.

"Sure, why not? It'll be dark in a few minutes, anyway. Look, there's even a road going up there." In the last grey light I could just make out a strand of lighter color winding up the dark pinnacle.

We went on through the town, and on the other side we found a dirt road going off in the direction of the castle. We'd been following it into the dark for about 15 minutes now.

Every time the road curved, we'd think, ahh, now, finally it'll start going up. But it never seemed to. "I don't think this is gonna make it," I said as we humped around another right bend. "In fact. . ."

Suddenly, we weren't alone. I *felt* the two black, hooded shapes before I really saw them—felt them in the pit of my stomach and the back of my neck. And when I finally realized what I was seeing, I didn't know whether to floor the gas pedal or the brake.

"Gaaaahh!" my wife remarked.

Not ol' super-cool, observant me, though. "It's okay," I said in a semi-strangled peep, trying to regain control of my bladder. "Ghosts don't have machine guns." These guys did.

"*Buenas tardes,*" I called to the apparitions.

"*Buena' tarde',*" they answered in the local accent. Following *Guardia Civil* custom, one unslung his machine gun and stood back to watch while the other came forward to exchange pleasantries.

"Is it possible to drive to the ruin on this road?" I asked him.

"The ruin! Yes, the road goes there . . . why do you want to go to the ruin?"

"We sleep in our truck, and we're looking for a place to pass the night. Nothing more."

"To pass the night!" He turned to grin at the other one, who slung his gun and came forward. "They spend the night in the ruin, Vicente!" the first guard told him. "In the *truck.*"

Vicente grinned at us and his buddy. "*Si?*"

"How much farther is it," I asked.

"Less than a kilometer. But it is very steep, *señor*. Perhaps you would rather spend the night here below. It is very pleasant here. *Muy tranquil.*" He shouted this last over a cataclysmic roar of wind and splatter of rain.

"Is there some reason why we should not go to the ruin?"

"Oh, no, *señor*. It is permitted, of course." He smiled and shrugged. "But most people do not go there. They say there is a curse. An old legend, you understand," he added, smiling broadly and crossing himself.

"Umm. Well, I think we'll try it anyway. Perhaps, *señores*, you will come to our camp later? For a glass of wine . . . or some hot coffee on such a bad night?"

They exchanged glances. "Many thanks, *señor*. But soon we go off duty."

"*Si, si, muy pronto!*" the other agreed, nodding a bit too vigorously. We thanked them, said good night and lurched onward into the gloom. Soon the road began to rise. And before we'd gone 200 yards, we were down to first gear, the old truck scrabbling frantically for footing in the mud and rocks. We lurched and jolted, stuff fell out of the cabinets in back, but we were still moving forward and up.

The road got steadily worse—and steeper. And we were still far below the castle. By now, though, I was determined to get to the thing, curses, steep roads or whatever. The Mighty Son of Moby Truck, however, was not, and we finally reached a piece that all its 40 ferocious horses couldn't manage.

"Well, we can't stay *here*. We won't sleep very well standing on our heads."

"Maybe we could back up it," I mused aloud. "Hell, I'm gonna go look at it first, though." I got out the flashlight, pulled a poncho over my head and walked up the road in the spattering, whipping darkness. The steep piece went up about 50 yards and then leveled off at a wide, flat area. A footpath, too steep for the car wound up the final slope to the ruin.

"There's a grand flat place up there," I told Jeffi when I got back to the truck. "Let's try backing up a bit and making an all-out charge."

"Is it all spooky and cursed up there?" Jeffi asked as we backed up.

"I couldn't tell—it was too dark. All I could see were glowing red eyes and luminous blue scaly things about the size of cows."

Our "all-out charge" (heroic, misleading phrase) did the trick. Wheezing, clattering, rear end going BAM! BAM! BAM! as it leaped and churned and slewed back and forth, we tumbled up and over the top. The truck sat level, idling quietly. And the little red generator light was on. I blipped the throttle. The light stayed on. Something jolted loose, probably. Why do these things always seem to happen at night, when you're being vigorously rained at? Well, it'd just have to wait until morning.

We had a fine, big dinner with lots of red wine and went to bed to listen to the drubbing rain. The truck rocked gently in the gusty wind.

"Do you believe that about the curse?" Jeffi asked sleepily.

ENCHANTED BUS

"Sure, why not? I stopped believing in reality after the last presidential election."

We slept the sleep of the righteous and just, curse or no, and during the night the rain stopped. We awoke to a bright, warm sun and an electric blue sky, and the view was just fantastic. Below us, the town was a glittering white splotch on the red-brown earth, and the mountains all around us gleamed in a new dusting of snow. And way off to the south, we could just see the blue haze of the sea.

"You want to go up to the ruin?" Jeffii asked after breakfast. "I think I'll go up there and sketch."

"Maybe soon. I've gotta see why this thing won't generate, first." While Jeffi roamed around the ruin, I tried to figure out the red light problem. Everything was connected and in place, and whatever the trouble was, it refused to be diagnosed by a test light or the scientifical spark-and-zapp techniques favored by under-equipped mechanics. Far as I could tell, the generator was working, and so was the regulator— I tried my spare one with no success. And everything was connected. But the generator light continued to glow fiercely red.

"Maybe it's cursed," Jeffi suggested when she came down from the castle. "Have you tried sacrificing a goat?"

"I was thinking more along the lines of a virgin. Hell, I can't do anything else up here. Let's go down to the town, maybe there's a generator shop there."

There was. A small, cluttered, gloomy place, but the guy had the necessary equipment, and he knew how to use it. After trying every test conceivable with an elderly roll-up console rig, he grunted to himself for a moment, then started pulling the generator. None of your mess-with-the-fan-shroud, take-out-the-carburetor business, either. He went right after the big nut that holds the generator shaft to the fan, and had the thing on the bench in three minutes flat. Clean it, test it, put in new brushes, test it again on the big machine. Perfect. Take out the regulator, test it. Perfect. Get a reading off the battery. Fine. Check every last wiring connection. Perfect.

Satisfied, the guy put it all back together. "Start it," he said finally.

I started it, staring intently at the generator light. The light stared redly, malevolently back at me.

"Puta," the guy said softly, peering at the light. He went away mumbling, came back with a voltmeter/ammeter and started testing it again. Everything checked out. But the red light glowed and no current seemed to be getting anywhere. The guy said some very unscientific things about the breeding habits of Germans. It didn't help.

"I do not understand, señor. It is not possible, this." We studied the engine silently for a moment. "No es posible," he said again, shaking his head.

"I thought at first that something was loose," I offered. "The road was very rough and the car was bouncing badly. We were on the old dirt road up to the ruin when it first . . ."

"¿La ruina!?" the guy yelped, looking at me like I'd offered him violence. "You went to the ruin? With your car? Ay, señor, why did you not say? La ruina! Dios!"

"Um, well . . ."

"You should have told me, señor! It would have saved much time—much work." He went to the front of the shop, looked furtively out and then shut the doors. "You must now go to Don Manolo, señor," he said in a whisper. "Tell no one, comprende? No one! Do not say it was I who sent you."

"Now, wait a minute. Let's start over again . . ."

"No, señor, there is nothing to say. You must go now—immediately to Don Manolo." He glanced at the windows for spies, then knelt on the dusty flood. "The road to the ruin is here . . . and here, a few hundred meters in, is a road to the left. Turn onto this road and follow it. It will take you to Don Manolo."

He stood, spit on his dust map, crossed himself and rubbed it out with his foot.

"What do I owe you?"

"Nothing, señor. Go quickly!"

"Let me pay you for your time, at least—and for the new generator brushes."

"Very well, a hundred pesetas. Quickly, señor, I beg you. Remove your car from my shop!" He squirmed and danced and screwed up his face like I was keeping him from the john, so I laid a hundred pesetas on him, started the truck and backed out of the shop.

"Señor! Señor!" The guy came running out. "Take these with you!" He threw the old generator brushes into the truck and scurried back to the shop, closing the doors behind him.

"Far out," I remarked to my wife. "Let's go see Don Manolo. This is getting wilder by the minute!"

The other dirt road wound and bumped through the dusty hills for about two kilometers, then petered out into a track. We heaved and lurched along, slower now, for another kilometer.

"You ever get the feeling you're involved in a massive put-on?" I asked Jeffi. "I don't think this track goes anywhere." We stopped. Ahead, the track faded into a rocky path.

"Umm . . ." Jeffi said, staring to the left. "Umm . . ." I looked; to our left, across a dusty yard, was a small white house with a man sitting in the doorway. He was smiling at us.

"Was that house there all the time?" I wondered aloud.

"The hell with that," said my wife. "Is it there now?"

"I'll ask the man."

I got out of the truck and approached the house. The man stood up and stretched his back, still smiling. He was about five-ten, slender, maybe 45 or 50, and dressed in the usual white shirt without collar and shapless, dusty black suit. Ordinary. But his face was not. Brown and weathered with high, strong cheekbones, it was seamed and creased into permanent lines, as if he had spent his whole life being vastly amused about something, and the hot Andalusian sun had cured his leathery face into a permanent smile. His teeth were even and white, and his black eyes sparkled.

"Don Manolo?"

"Yes, I am Manolo," he said extending his hand. "Welcome. I have been expecting you. Ah! Please ask the señora if she will join us for some refreshment." He turned on his heel and went into the little house.

He came out carrying three glasses and a bottle of dark red wine. I introduced him to Jeffi and he bowed low. "My house is your house, *señora*. I am honored." Charmed ol' Jeffi right up the wall, he did.

We sat on a rough bench, Don Manolo sat in his doorway and we drank to each other's health a time or two.

"So, *señor*—your *coche* does not function correctly?"

"The problem is in the *dynamo*, Don Manolo. Or so it appears."

"No matter," he said with a smile. He drained his glass, stretched slowly upright, took a crooked stick from beside the door and walked to the center of his dusty yard. A brown and white goat came out of the house and walked over toward him. With the stick, Don Manolo began to scratch a big circle in the dust. Then, while the goat stood and watched, he drew another. Soon, five big intersecting circles had been drawn, making a design some 20 feet across. Don Manolo and the goat went and stood silently in the center for a moment. *One* of them was mumbling something, and from where I sat, I'd have sworn it was the goat.

"Now *señor*, please drive your car here to the center of the design."

I backed the truck to the place indicated, got out, and watched Don Manolo repair the circles where the tires had crossed them. "Now we must wait a time. Come! Some more wine!"

We sat on the bench again and watched while the goat began to shuffle in a slow, wide circle around Don Manolo's design and my truck.

"Uh, Don Manolo. . .is it permitted to ask. . .uh, *Que pasa*? What's happening here?"

Don Manolo shrugged and smiled. "It is simple, *señor*—you got too close to the old citadel, and your *coche* has fallen under the Curse of Iron. We must now remove that curse and replace it with a charm. More wine?"

"A curse, you say? What kind of curse?"

Don Manolo laughed softly. "Yes, a curse. But not so terrible a curse. The people here frighten easily, you understand. No, the curse will not harm people, *señor*. It harms only metal." Don Manolo poured more wine, then settled back against the door jamb.

"Many hundreds of years ago," Don Manolo continued, "when the citadel was near the end of its time of glory, the caliph who ruled it had a great and powerful wizard—the seventh son of a seventh son of a seventh son. Those were decadent times, *señor*, and one must assume that the caliph's faith in Allah's protection was. . .impaired, let us say. For when the lookouts called the approach of the armies of the reconquest who had come in all their armor to take the citadel, the caliph ordered his wizard to cast a protective spell. Allah's intercession, it is said, was sought only as an afterthought.

"So the wizard, not content with a mere spell (which could be broken by any journeyman sorcerer), threw a curse over the whole citadel and the area just below it. This was the Curse of Iron. It rendered any metal in its presence useless, and the caliph found to his amazement that his scimitar would not even cut butter. Having demonstrated the power of the Curse of Iron, the wizard then ordered that all metal in the citadel be brought into his presence. And when all of the metal and armor and arrows and weapons had been brought to the throne room, the Wizard charmed them. . .and the delighted caliph now found that his scimitar, and all the other weapons in the citadel would slash through solid iron without dulling or breaking. And when the crusaders attacked, their armor and their weapons failed them, and they withdrew in defeat."

Don Manolo paused to sip at his wine, and I found myself gazing at the distant ruin, which glowed deep red in the afternoon sun.

"They were a great people, *señor*. But the tide that carried them to glory had turned, as it must, in time, for all great peoples. And as their spirit ebbed, they became quarrelsome and evil and cruel, and they fought among themselves. The crusaders had only to wait. In time, the citadel fell from within and flung open its gates to the inevitable. Crumbling walls and a lingering curse are all that remain."

The goat, which had stopped its roundabout shuffling, came over to Jeffi and nibbled her sleeve. Then it stood with lidded eyes like an overgrown tomcat while she scratched its ears.

"And you, Don Manolo?" I asked, "you know how to remove the Curse of Iron?"

"Yes. And I also know how to place the antidote—the Charm of Ahmed El Fkih. That was the wizard's name. And I am seventh son of a seventh son of a seventh son. . . it is many generations, *señor*, but it leads directly back to Ahmed El Fkih himself. And with it has come the Vision and the Power." Don Manolo said something to the goat in what I'll swear was Arabic. The goat turned and looked at him, then went back to the important business of getting its ears scratched.

"It is done, *señor*. Your *coche* will now function. Also, it is protected from future harm by the Charm of Ahmed El Fkih."

I got in, twisted the key, the engine whirred alive and the little red generator light blinked out.

Don Manolo wanted no money. "Your company has repaid me," he said with a smile. He glanced at the goat. "And Ahmed El Fkih is sorry for your trouble and for the one-hundred *pesetas* you spent in town. Also, he thanks the *señora* for scratching his ears." The goat nodded gravely.

"Oh, Jesus Christ," Jeffi whispered, looking wide-eyed at the goat.

"*Adios.*" Don Manolo and Ahmed El Fkih turned and walked into the house.

(News item: The absolute world land speed record for '63 VW trucks was set over three flying kilometers of dirt road in Spain on April 15th of 1971 at 4:32 p.m.)

"Keep a sharp eye for guys in white with butterfly nets," I told Jeffi as we boomed down the highway to Almeria. "And to hell with that Spanish red—let's get us a big bottle of cognac tonight."

And that ended it. . .sort of. Gradually, the memory got fuzzy around the edges and blurred about the middle, until

ENCHANTED BUS

it was finally classified down into our vast collection of Weird Trips and Funny Bits—like the night we got hopelessly lost in the rain and the dark and found that the "big mother rain puddle" that kept blocking our path was the Mediterranean. And by the time we got to Amsterdam, the glitter and stink of science and civilization had just about erased the event.

But one day in a Dutch campground I began to wonder. Something wasn't right. Or rather, everything was a little *too* right; the truck had never run better—it hadn't acted up, broken down or crapped out for almost two months— ever since that day in Spain. And this was not typical of our truck. There was always *something*.

Well, running right or not, the oil was still due for a change, and while I was at it, might as well do the valves and set the points too. So I put on my grubbies and scrootched under the car. . .

The feeling that something was amiss was not helped by the fact that I couldn't get the oil drain plug out. I pulled and strained and grunted and braced my feet and beat on it and swore at it in Tongues, but the nut would not come loose. Very well then; I would think about the problem while I did the valves.

I will spare you all the things I tried. Just suffice it to say that the locknuts on the rockers wouldn't come loose, either. And when I found that I couldn't even get the distributor cap off, I threw all my tools back under the seat, changed, collected my wife and headed into Amsterdam. There, we spent a fruitless but memorable hour and a half watching a team of five Dutch VW mechanics try to change the oil. Toward the end, the shop manager came forward with a sly little smile, carrying the Main Breaker Bar and the Great Ceremonial Cheater Pipe. We left them, finally, standing around in a little huddle thoughtfully regarding the stripped and mangled teeth of a 17-mm socket.

So at that point, we stopped trying to fight it. That oil's been in there for eight months now, and it's still fresh and clean. And the truck just never, ever, *ever* gives trouble!

Another thing we found—that truck also has a strange effect on parking meters; they stop running in its presence, and you can park for a month on ten cents. Cops can't give it tickets, either—pencils break and ball-points make a little "glurk!" noise and dispense all their ink at once, making the Man in Blue considerably bluer.

Strange, yes. But it surely is nice to know that your car will always get you there and back. *Always*. In fact the only drawback to owning that truck is the strange feeling you get when you lie in there on a dark night and think about it. Too, Jeffi occasionally has a recurring, mildly disturbing dream where this goat follows her around asking for cigarettes in Arabic. When she gives him one, he eats it.

But our time here is coming to an end soon. We'll have to sell the truck in the spring and turn our minds to other things. Hey, that reminds me—you know anybody coming over here who might want a very reliable, maintenance-free VW truck? I'll take $1000 for it. Yeah, sure, I know that's steep for a '63. But where else you gonna get a 5000-year, 50,000,000,000-mile guarantee?

A VW is what you make it. The pick-up can easily be modified to fit the particular requirements of your business.

With sides down, it's a flatbed truck. (No wheel wells in the way.) It can be had without sides and tailgate, a lower cost option.

With bows and tarpaulin (an optional extra) it's a covered van with 161 cu. ft. of sheltered space (plus the 20-sq.-ft. locker).

This VW Pick-Up has been modified for use as a glazier's truck. Some owners turn it into a stake truck. Others, a utility truck.

A VW is adaptable. The 170 cubic feet of load space can easily be modified to fit the needs of almost every businessman.

A cleaner installs racks for hanging garments clear of the floor.

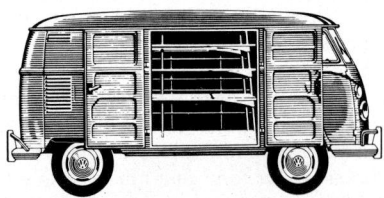

A baker can install a system of adjustable shelves or tray-racks.

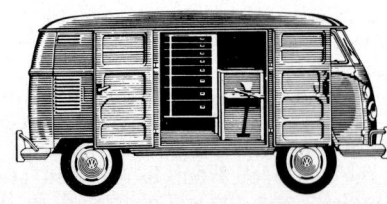

A repairman can build-in binned storage space for tools, parts.